Cambridge Elements ☰

Elements in Travel Writing
edited by
Nandini Das
University of Oxford
Tim Youngs
Nottingham Trent University

WRITING TUDOR EXPLORATION

Richard Eden and West Africa

Matthew Dimmock
University of Sussex

CAMBRIDGE
UNIVERSITY PRESS

CAMBRIDGE
UNIVERSITY PRESS

University Printing House, Cambridge CB2 8BS, United Kingdom

One Liberty Plaza, 20th Floor, New York, NY 10006, USA

477 Williamstown Road, Port Melbourne, VIC 3207, Australia

314–321, 3rd Floor, Plot 3, Splendor Forum, Jasola District Centre, New Delhi – 110025, India

103 Penang Road, #05–06/07, Visioncrest Commercial, Singapore 238467

Cambridge University Press is part of the University of Cambridge.

It furthers the University's mission by disseminating knowledge in the pursuit of education, learning, and research at the highest international levels of excellence.

www.cambridge.org
Information on this title: www.cambridge.org/9781009045858
DOI: 10.1017/9781009047005

© Matthew Dimmock 2022

First published 2022

A catalogue record for this publication is available from the British Library.

ISBN 978-1-009-04585-8 Paperback
ISSN 2632-7090 (online)
ISSN 2632-7082 (print)

Writing Tudor Exploration

Richard Eden and West Africa

Elements in Travel Writing

DOI: 10.1017/9781009047005
First published online: July 2022

Matthew Dimmock
University of Sussex

Author for correspondence: Matthew Dimmock, M.Dimmock@sussex.ac.uk

Abstract: Richard Eden's *Decades* (1555) has long been recognised as a landmark in the translation and circulation of information concerning the Americas in England. What is often overlooked in Eden's book is the presence of the first two Tudor voyage accounts to have been committed to print, assembled in haste and added late in the printing process. Both concern English commercial ventures to the West African coast, undertaken despite vehement Portuguese protests and in the midst of the profound alteration of the Marian succession. Both are complex, contradictory, and innovative experiments in generic form and content. *Writing Tudor Exploration* closely examines Eden's assembly and framing of these accounts, engaging with issues of material culture, travel writing, new knowledge, race, and the negotiation of political and religious change. In the process it repositions West Africa and Eden at the heart of a lost history of early English expansionism.

Keywords: Tudor England, trade, travel writing, Guinea/West Africa, Richard Eden

ISBNs: 9781009045858 (PB), 9781009047005 (OC)
ISSNs: 2632-7090 (online), 2632-7082 (print)

Contents

Preface

I was desyred by certeyne my frendes to make summe mention of these viages, that sum memorie therof myght remayne to owr posteritie if eyther iniquitie of tyme consumynge all thinges, or ignoraunce creepynge in by barbarousnesse and contempte of knoweleage, shulde hereafter bury in oblivion so woorthy attemptes.

(Eden, 1555: 343r)

As is often the case, the original conception of this Element was quite different to the end result. Long interested in early modern literature of travel and exploration, I was keen to look in detail at the origins and form of such accounts: *Writing Tudor Exploration* is therefore concerned with the writing produced as part of commercially or colonially minded enterprises that sought to open up new geographies and/or new markets, often requiring substantial time in unknown lands or waters. However, this was originally imagined as a project focussed on the explosion of English voyage writing that appeared in the near decade that separated the two momentous Elizabethan circumnavigations of the globe, the first undertaken by Francis Drake (1577–80) and the second by Thomas Cavendish (1586–8). Aside from a few isolated earlier examples, that period seemed to represent the beginnings of a distinctively English approach to such writing. It certainly offers a wealth of activity and material, encompassing the last of the Frobisher voyages in search of the North-West Passage, Edward Fenton's abortive voyage to China, Humphrey Gilbert's claiming of Newfoundland, Arthur Barlowe's reconnaissance of the North American coast, Richard Grenville's colonising of Roanoke, John Davis's three voyages to Greenland and Labrador also in search of the North-West Passage, and Drake's later South American adventures, as well as the circumnavigations themselves.

These voyages – crucial to what Robert Brenner has called Elizabethan England's 'expansionary thrust' (Brenner, 2003: 12) – required an extraordinary mobilisation of credit, resources, and people; they were also an unprecedented and vital textual endeavour. Furthermore the form itself was still unstable at this point. The later dominance of the first-person, eyewitness report was not yet inevitable, and it was only one among many early forms variously employing verse and prose, sometimes in chronicle or epistolary formats: what William Sherman describes as 'complex rhetorical strategies' (Sherman, 2002: 17). Similarly the travel collection had yet to be established as the pre-eminent print format, with some accounts published individually and others remaining in manuscript, before most were drawn together in a carefully edited demonstration of English imperial vigour in Richard Hakluyt's *Principal Navigations*, the first edition of which appeared in 1589. These collective uncertainties indicate that before Hakluyt this was a precarious genre in search of form and audience.

Inevitably my search for the beginnings of Tudor English sea-voyage writing began to lead me earlier. Any such study needed to start with the compendious effort led initially by Richard Eden to gather together materials relating to the distinct Spanish and Portuguese colonial projects in the Americas, West Africa, and Southeast Asia that were increasingly becoming available by the middle of the sixteenth century. The world as imagined from peripheral England was in the process of profound change, and Eden attempted to chart, manage, and identify the potential advantages to be gained from such changes. I was dimly aware that, as part of that effort, Eden had drawn together some brief accounts of English commercial excursions to what he and his readership understood as 'Guinea', a region incorporating a swathe of the West African coastline from modern-day Senegal to Nigeria, and I knew something of those accounts through their (misleading, it turns out) reproduction by Hakluyt.[1] Having previously undertaken some research into Edwardian expansionist policies, led particularly by John Dudley, Duke of Northumberland, and their significant influence on later Elizabethan ideas, I also had an idea of the importance of Eden's work as part of that project and the interconnection of these West African voyages with near-simultaneous English efforts in search of the North-East Passage and along North American coasts. As a result I was interested to see how those accounts Eden included in his book were framed in the context of the wider intellectual and practical work underway in England in the early 1550s, as well as any specific connections that might be made to the writing that followed.

What I found when looking closely at Eden's volume changed my sense of this project and of the bigger intellectual questions I had intended to ask. The two English voyages to Guinea that he gathered and reproduced are the first of their kind, but they are also profoundly odd documents. All of the intercon- nected debates about form, politics, coloniality, race, and new ideas about the globe that I had seen in the voyage writing of more than two decades later suffused these texts and the idiosyncratic ways Eden chose to present them. At the same time they were shaped by the immediate political and cultural contexts in which they emerged, most immediately by Marian regime change and the rapid shifts in geopolitical and religious policy that accompanied it. As a result Eden's detailed knowledge of Spanish and Portuguese voyage writing informed his approach but could sometimes lead to unacknowledged mimicry, sometimes to outright rejection, in an uneven stumbling towards a redefinition of the terms in which ideological underpinnings, as well as cultural and racial difference, were articulated and Indigenous peoples depicted. His thorough, humanistic

---

[1] I have flagged Guinea here as a Christian European construct; that acknowledged, subsequent use will dispense with the quotation marks.

grounding in the texts of antiquity as well as those of contemporary geographers meant that Eden's English Guinea accounts become a forum in which he could tussle with Pliny, Ptolemy, and Herodotus, testing the limits of their theoretical positions against recent work, most prominently that of Gemma Frisius (Jemme Reinerszoon), and against the empirical data collated in the English eyewitness accounts. The results can be contradictory but offer an exhilarating sense of new knowledge, strategies, and mercantile policies, as well as new narrative possibilities, coming into being.

In my epigraph Eden reflects upon the need to remember these voyages. That imperative meant something very different when he was writing than it did for later generations of readers. His book appeared at a moment when the achievements of Edward VI's reign looked in danger of total erasure as England was pulled into a Hapsburg orbit with Mary I's 1554 marriage to Philip, King of Naples and Sicily (and later Spain). Eden's compulsion to fix these achievements in a collective national memory was a desperate attempt at preservation in the face of political expunction. By the time elements of Eden's book were reproduced by Richard Willes in 1577, or by Richard Hakluyt in 1589 and 1598–1600, the same words had become an exhortation to record, gather, and continue what was now an Elizabethan expansionist project. As well as the meaning, the identity of that voice was sometimes lost in reproduction, with neither Willes nor Hakluyt crediting this opening passage to Eden, and uncertainty over the sources of the two voyages has allowed Eden's contribution to be overlooked. His achievement has, as a result, often been accorded to others, and this has been reflected in the scholarly field, where the multinational, uncategorisable nature of Eden's work has led to its eclipse by Hakluyt's nationally focussed anthology, particularly since the latter's nineteenth-century canonisation.[2] Although his version of these two voyages is the only historical source for the earliest sustained English engagements with West Africa – the importance of which for Tudor expansionism has itself often been overlooked – Eden tends to be castigated by specialists for his partiality and perceived inaccuracies, or ignored entirely. With a few important exceptions there has consequently been relatively little scholarship on his editing of the accounts or how we might read them in the context of changing English conceptions of the world at this crucially important juncture.[3]

All of these factors explain how this Element came to be about Eden and his book. Although it does recover a lost history it is not intended as the kind of memorialisation he claimed to be undertaking but is instead a detailed

---

[2] In contrast to Hakluyt, whose work has seen considerable critical attention, the only modern edition of Eden is Arber, 1885.

[3] See in particular Alsop, 1992; Hair and Alsop, 1992; Hair, 1997; Fuller, 2006.

interrogation of the strikingly different forms he adopts in order to present these earliest English sea voyages in print. How Eden responded to complex circumstances and balanced the needs of different readers plays a prominent role. I owe a considerable debt to the general editors of the Cambridge Elements Studies in Travel Writing series, Nandini Das and Tim Youngs, for the invitation to submit this Element and for their patience throughout. I am also very grateful to the two anonymous readers for Cambridge University Press who made some very helpful suggestions and gave me much to think about. For always stimulating conversation and encouragement I'd like to express my particular gratitude to Andrew Hadfield, whose expertise and good humour have been invaluable, but also to Jerry Brotton, Steven Gunn, Tomasz Kowalczyk, Ladan Niayesh, Tom Roberts, and Jyotsna Singh, as well as to medieval and early modern colleagues and students at the Sussex Centre for Early Modern and Medieval Studies. In helping me to overcome what Eden, with characteristic eloquence, described as the 'iniquitie of tyme consumynge all thinges', I owe special thanks to my family: Tierney, Betty, and Oren. This Element is dedicated to them.

A Note on Dating and Modernisation

Although in most cases the early modern English year began on 25 March, where relevant I have altered the dates so that the year begins on the previous 1 January in line with contemporary practice. I have silently modernised some elements of early modern spelling (i/j, u/v, the long s, ligatures) for reasons of clarity but have otherwise remained as close as possible to the original texts. For West African place names, which can vary considerably between early modern and twenty-first-century usage, I have given both forms where available.

Introduction: Writing Tudor Exploration

Writings about English voyages of trade and exploration did not begin neatly. They did not emerge, generically fully formed, in the ready-made and extensive 'library of the sea' provided by the two editions of the younger Richard Hakluyt's *Principal Navigations* (Quinn, 1974: 221). There is no straightforward line to be drawn, for instance, from medieval pilgrimage accounts or the ubiquitous fourteenth-century *Travels* purportedly by John Mandeville to Thomas Ellis's *A true report of the third and last voyage into Meta Incognita* (1578), written by a 'rude sailor' untrained in the arts of 'Minerva's Court' (Ellis, 1578: A3r). Instead the earliest published accounts of Tudor voyages are literally afterthoughts, slashed and distorted by the forces that brought them into existence. This Element is an attempt to recover those initial circumstances and to begin to trace their influence on the rapid development of a form that within a few decades had become so well known that its mere mention summoned up tangled and contradictory associations with tall tales, prolixity, and tedium.

Later voyage narratives were in many respects idiosyncratically English and developed, as I will show, in response to uniquely English circumstances and concerns. Nevertheless they initially emerged in thrall to evolving Portuguese, Spanish, and, to a lesser extent, Italian and French models. This was a genre that from the beginning did not quite know what it was or what it should be. Was the letter the most effective way of communicating and authorising accounts of Christian European 'discovery', following the celebrated examples produced by Columbus (from 1493) and Cortés (from 1522) and widely disseminated?[4] Did the subjective taint of the epistolary undermine the new knowledge these accounts sought to codify despite the first-hand authenticity associated with the form? Under such pressures these initial letters rapidly began to morph into different shapes in the hands of subsequent editors and travellers. Columbus's letters were transformed into poetry in Giuliano Dati's *Lettera dell'isole che ha trovato nuovamente il Re di Spagna* (1493); letters reformed into reports featured prominently in the early *De orbe nove decades*, written by the Italian historian working in Spain Pietro Martire d'Anghiera (Peter Martyr) between 1511 and 1535 and published across Europe thereafter (see Brennan, 1996/7: 227–45). This text was then partly translated into English by Richard Eden for his 1555 edition, itself another kind of generic puzzle.

Variants of the letter also lingered in the equally direct but less obviously subjective *relación* (relation) template used by Francisco de Xeres and Pedro Pizarro when narrating the conquest of Peru, and in Jacques Cartier's 1545 account of Canada (de Xerez, 1534; Cartier, 1545). *Relación* would later mingle with *commentarios* (commentary) in Álvar Núñez Cabeza de Vaca's account of North America (de Vaca, 1555) and gain political and moral urgency in Bartholomé de las Casas's *Brevisima relación de la desctrucción de las Indias* (1552). The ghostly presence of the eyewitness letter remains but is suppressed in the reframing of first-hand sea voyage accounts as *historia* – drawing on a different generic authority, that of the earlier chronicle history – that probably began with Fernandez de Oviedo y Valdes's two volumes on the Indies, *La natural historia* (1526) and *La historia general* (1535). That model then appeared with much greater frequency in the 1550s, with the publication of *historia* relating voyages of conquest to both east and west, including widely

---

[4] The first extant printed copy of a Columbus letter was that produced by Pedro Posa in Barcelona in 1493. Eleven editions appeared in different European languages in the same year. The first of Cortés's letters to Charles V is no longer extant, but the second and third letters were printed in Seville in 1522 and 1523.

read and translated volumes by Fernão Lopes de Castanheda (1551–61), Francisco López de Gómara (1552), and Augustine de Zerate (1555). In England its popularity was clearly a factor in Richard Willes's repackaging of Eden's translation of the *Decades* as *The history of travayle in the East and West Indies* (1577).

Other models simultaneously emerged in response to the challenge of conceptualising this *mundus novus*, this reordered world. New cosmographies sought to fuse classical geographies with new geographies such as those by Boemus (1520) and Münster (1550), both widely read in England, as well as the articulation of new horizons through the long-established *itinerario*, exemplified in Ludovico di Varthema's 1510 volume of the same name (and in Linschoten's celebrated later text). A maritime focus begins to appear with a sequence of *voyage et navigation* texts, such as Antonio Pigafetta's 1525 account of Magellan's circumnavigation. Martyr's *Decades* was one among a number of collections of travel narratives that brought together such accounts in a polyvocal whole: other examples include Francanzano Montalboddo's *Paesi Novamente Retrovati* (1507) and Johan Hüttich and Simon Gryneus's *Novus orbis* (1532). As the titles of all three demonstrate, these were collections focussed primarily on the wonders of the Americas. Even more influential, especially in an English context, was Gian Battista Ramusio's hugely popular and influential *Delle navigazioni e viaggi*, the first volume of which appeared in 1550. Across what were eventually three volumes, Ramusio gathered eighty-two voyage narratives that for the first time moved beyond the Americas to cover the entirety of the extra-European world as it was currently understood. Throughout he sought to foreground the authority of the eyewitness and obscure 'his own editorial interventions' (Small, 2012: 46) in an approach that would exert a profound influence on subsequent writers and editors, most obviously Richard Hakluyt and the two editions of his *Principal Navigations*.

Many different generic models were therefore in play in the first half of the sixteenth century, each offering an ostensibly distinct vehicle for the dispersal of new geographical information as it haphazardly emerged from under the 'severe check' of Iberian powers who had distinct expansionist agendas (Faldini, 1992: 52). Yet, as this initial summary demonstrates, generic labels are of only limited use: what appears to be solid can dissolve under closer scrutiny. Voices coalesce and divide; history becomes navigation and travel account becomes reflective *discoursi*; tensions remain between appealing to specialist and general readers, between the indistinct methods of the author and of the editor, and between eyewitness reportage and literary invention. Although Ramusio (and later Hakluyt) presented their voyage texts apparently unmediated, they were both interventionist editors, shaping and selecting what they included, interjecting and authorising to different ends. In his *Historia*, of which the first eight volumes (of ten) were published in Lisbon between 1551 and his death in 1559, de Castanheda lightly finessed a synoptic central narrative that drew together numerous travel accounts and documentary sources, but he did not conceal its polyvocality. As its English translator Nicholas Litchfield later noted, this was not a straightforward history: it 'containeth much varietie of matter, very profitable for all navigators, and not unpleasant to the Readers', an idea he elaborated in his dedication to Francis Drake (de Castanheda, 1582: title page). A different approach was adopted by Oviedo in his *La natural historia de las Indias*, in which he sought to emulate Ptolemy and Pliny, and for which extensive oral and written sources 'were personally collected, revised and then transposed into summarizing narration that established his authority as author' (de la Rosa, 2002: 80). Unlike Castanheda, whose approach was that of an editor assembling fragments, for Oviedo it was the travails of the individual author-collector that sublimated disparate sources into autoptic truth; he cast doubt on the methods of others and rather disingenuously reflected, 'I do not write with the authority of an historian or poet, but as an eyewitness' (quoted in de la Rosa, 2002: 80).

Written accounts by eyewitnesses to these new worlds were, however, hard to come by in England in the first half of the sixteenth century. The north-westward voyages of John and later Sebastian Cabot in search of a passage to Asia left only fragmentary records and no surviving authorial account (see Williamson ed., 1962), and the letters associated with Robert Thorne, although circulating in manuscript, were not printed until their inclusion in Hakluyt's *Divers Voyages* (1582). The evidence of other early voyages survives only thanks to Hakluyt's efforts in collecting oral testimony and disparate letters for his *Principal Navigations* (1589). Active English engagement in the Newfoundland fishery throughout this period has also left few documentary traces (Cell, 1969: 3–21). Eyewitness testimony was certainly sought after: John Rastell's play *A new interlude and a mery of the nature of the iiii elements* (*c.*1519) manufactures that authority in the fictional character of Experyens, who merrily asserts that 'Ryght farre, syr, I haue rydden and gone, / And seen straunge thynges many one, / In Affryk, Europe, and Ynde' (Rastell, 1979: ll. 669–71). A central part of his didactic periplus of the known world is a reflection on the geography and peoples of the Americas, which he laments could have been English had English mariners taken the opportunity shown them by the Cabots. Gesturing to a chart, he instructs his audience that:

> This See is called the great Occyan,
> So great it is that never man
> Coude tell it sith the worlde began,

Tyll nowe, within this twenty yere,
Westwarde be founde new landes
That we never harde tell of before this
By wrytynge nor other meanys
Yet many nowe have ben there.
(Rastell, 1979: ll. 733–40)

Rastell had considerable knowledge of the subject – John Bale described him as *cosmographus* (Rastell, 1979: 10) – and drew upon a number of sources for his American material, most of which were themselves cosmographies, prominently Martin Waldseemüller's *Cosmographiae Introductio* and its accompanying map (1507). The frustration evident in Rastell's play at English tardiness and their exclusion from the 'many' that now frequent these 'new landes' resurfaces decades later in the next work concerning such matters to appear in print, Richard Eden's partial translation of Sebastian Münster's *Cosmographia*, which he titled *The treatyse of the newe India with other new founde landes and islandes, aswell eastwarde as westwarde* (1553). Eden was not 'utterlye ignoraunt' of cosmography, as he self-depreciatingly acknowledged in his dedicatory epistle to that 'great prince' John Dudley, Duke of Northumberland (Eden, 1553: aa2r), then unofficial Lord Protector of the young Edward VI. He intended to use his knowledge to exhort his countrymen to engage in the 'noble enterprises' underway elsewhere in Christian Europe. Look 'in this smal boke as in a little glasse', he wrote, and 'see some cleare light' that by the example of others the English might learn 'how to behave them selves & direct theyr viage to their most co[m]moditie' (Eden, 1553: aa3r–aa3v).

Although presented as a personal enterprise Eden's first book was the public-facing component of a concerted effort, led by Northumberland, to plot and justify English commercial and colonial expansion in response to domestic economic malaise (Brenner, 2003: 5–11). Eden had been one of a number of scholars and merchant adventurers – notably Clement Adams, William Buckley, John Dee, Leonard and Thomas Digges, Robert Recorde, and Ralph Robinson – loosely assembled to work to that end. The translation of Spanish and Portuguese examples was a key part of this strikingly ambitious but short-lived enterprise, and Eden's selection from Münster included the voyages of Columbus, Vespucci, and Magellan, as well as material from Portuguese voyages eastward. Like earlier examples it was a generic hybrid, mingling first-hand accounts with natural history, mythology, and poetry, but it was nonetheless influential, in part because its appearance was so well timed: the book was printed just as the Company of Merchant Adventurers, with Northumberland's patronage, was despatching a voyage in search of the North-West Passage under the command of Hugh Willoughby and Richard Chancellor.

Eden thus became the primary conduit for the miscellaneous, polyvocal, generically diverse material on the expanding world reaching England by the middle of the century. This made him the obvious person to edit and reproduce the first equivalent voyage accounts produced by English mariners and merchants to appear in print. Their subject is less obvious. The intense focus of English commercial efforts on the north-west with the 1553 Willoughby and Chancellor voyage was widely known, and Eden certainly shared a sense of this and subsequent northern voyages as 'heroic national endeavours' (Fuller, 2006: 25). Although Willoughby and two ships were lost, Chancellor returned having established trading privileges with the Russian court of Ivan IV, prompting the establishment of the Muscovy Company, which was granted its charter on 26 February 1555.[5] One might therefore expect this enterprise to have generated the first published account of English exploration, and in its aftermath Eden certainly gathered together a body of contextual material to accommodate such a text. However the narrative went elsewhere: he explained that he 'shall not neede here to describe that viage, forasuche as the same is largely and faythfully written in the Laten tongue by that lerned young man Clement Adams', a royal tutor, who had 'receaved it at the moutht of the sayde Richard Chanceler' (Eden, 1555: 256r). Now lost, this initial version of Adams's 'Anglorum navigatio ad Muscovitas' appears to have been written specifically for presentation to Mary I in 1554 (see Hakluyt, 1589: 292), a tributary mode that was itself an established subgenre of early exploration writing. Eden's remarks suggest some wider circulation, but it would not appear in print until included with an accompanying English translation in Hakluyt's *Principal Navigations* (Hakluyt, 1589: 270–92). Intriguingly, Adams's text demonstrates none of the narrative tricks, twists, and turns that characterise Eden's Guinea material, suggesting that publication exerted a considerable influence on form.

Instead the 'earliest printed accounts of English voyages to any part of the overseas world', indeed, 'the earliest detailed accounts of any long-distance English voyage now extant' (Hair and Alsop, 1992: 1), came from a direction that seems to have surprised even Eden, as well as many twenty-first-century readers. They concern Guinea, an area that had, aside from Ramusio's *Delle navigazioni e viaggi*, barely featured in early voyage collections largely fixated on the west. West Africa was a region similarly unfamiliar to the majority of Eden's first readers, but it was central to English commercial ambitions. A network of English merchants, drawing on extensive experience in Iberian

---

[5] Eden refers to Chancellor as an 'excellent yonge man' who was 'no lesse lerned in all mathematicall sciences then an expert pylotte' and thus an epitome of the new technologies required of the professional mariner of the sixteenth century (Eden, 1555: 251v). Hakluyt reproduced this endorsement to preface Adams's text (Hakluyt, 1589: 270).

trade and the expertise of Sebastian Cabot (whom Eden knew well and had attended on his deathbed), were with royal encouragement seeking to extend their reach, generating a series of interconnected initiatives (Dalton, 2016: 182–4). Almost all of the investors in this early Guinea trade would also become charter members of the Muscovy Company, for instance, indicating the close correspondence of the two spheres in the wider Edwardian expansionist enterprise (Willan, 1953: 26–7). English ships had been attracted to West Africa from at least the 1530s – if not earlier – by relatively easy access, tales of vast Portuguese profits, and a desire for luxury commodities (see Hair and Alsop, 1992: 5–6; Brooks, 2018: 122–35).[6] It was also a key staging point for journeys on to South America. Eden's overarching concern with the encouragement of English commerce and navigation through, around, between, and in spite of Spanish and Portuguese dominance, developing what I am calling a 'para-imperial' model, meant that these accounts became curious exemplars: they are at once celebrations of English commercial success, warnings against English cupidity, lessons in the value of specific goods, and engagements with classical geographies. With them Eden sought above all to effect real change in his readers and the wider culture.

The close examination of his reproduction of the first two English voyage accounts that concerns this Element demonstrates that Eden was more than simply translator and editor and that these accounts deserve a wider prominence in all their complexity. It indicates the importance of Guinea and shows how Eden was as innovative with such material as – perhaps even more than – many of his celebrated European contemporaries, and how on the level of narrative, form, and format he had a profound influence on those English writers and editors who followed him. I begin with an entry into the wider collection, his *Decades*, and his vision of the volume as the beginning of a paper monument, an archive of English expansionism. Following this notion, and Eden's own preoccupations, each of the following sections is similarly themed by its dominant element: first paper, then gold, and finally ivory.

1 Paper: Eden's *Decades*

Ostensibly a translation of the first three of Peter Martyr's *Decades*, Eden's *The Decades of the Newe Worlde or West India* (1555) appeared in the middle of the 1550s, a crucial decade for gathering and rethinking voyage writing as a mass of Iberian material began to reach wider European audiences for the first time. The task of translating and interpreting it was a challenging and controversial one.

---

[6] An earlier voyage had been planned in 1481, although it is not clear if it took place in the face of Portuguese objections: see Fuller, 2006: 13 n. 5.

Under the influence of Ramusio Eden loosely incorporated Martyr's structure but augmented his material with further translations including extracts from Oviedo, López de Gómara, Pigafetta on Magellan, as well as material from Paulo Giovio, reference to Cabot, and an account of Russia, a region (as Eden notes) crucial to mid-century English expansionist ambitions. More miscellaneous even than its most heterogeneous Spanish, Portuguese, and Italian predecessors, or his own *Treatyse*, the palimpsest-like unfixity of Eden's collection also reflects the complex political, commercial, and devotional circumstances of its creation. For some it is a 'badly organised book' that is nonetheless 'readable' (Gwyn, 1984: 29), and it features a lengthy prefatory address to the reader that, as Andrew Hadfield has recognised, is 'beset with anxiety' (Hadfield, 1998: 86). With the early death of Edward VI in 1553, the downfall and then execution of Northumberland later the same year, and the dispersal of his supporters, many of whom chose Protestant exile rather than accommodation with Mary I's restored Roman Catholicism, Eden was faced with a stark choice. He opted to remain in England, transferring his allegiance, skills, and raw materials to the service of the new regime.

Northumberland's global mercantile ambitions had been underpinned by a Protestantised surplus theory of international commerce that would later be prominently espoused by Thomas Smith, with whom Eden was closely associated.[7] That theory is encapsulated in the letter Edward VI had sent with Chancellor and Willoughby to the king of Cathay in 1553, a letter Eden reproduced in Latin and English: in it Edward argued that, 'For god of heaven and earth, greatly provydynge for mankynde, wolde not that al thynges shulde bee founde in one region, to thende that one shuld have neede of an other, that by this meanes frendshippe myght bee establysshed amonge all men, and every one seeke to gratifie all' (Eden, 1555: 308v). Eden now had to shift from this irenic position of 'universall amitie', with its evangelical certainties and conviction of England's place as a divine agent in the world, to an active endorsement of the Spanish imperial project, which required some ideological contortions. From its beginning Eden presents his book as a necessary monument to all Christian imperial achievements; quoting Cicero he asserts the noble mind of man and the importance of 'sume honest thynge' which 'not onely leaveth amonge men a memorie of his immortall nature, but also engendereth the lyke affection in other that delyte to see and heare such thinges as are commendable in theyr predicessours' (Eden, 1555: A1r). For 'trewe and permanent glory' can only proceed from 'such monumentes as brynge sume great and notable commoditie & profite to the

---

[7] The connection is well established: Smith had been Eden's tutor at Cambridge and had a copy of the *Decades* in his library. See Gwyn, 1984: 16.

life of men' (Eden, 1555: A1v). So classical and Christian examples – the tomb of Mausolus, the Temple of Solomon – are to be celebrated, whereas 'the hugious heapes of stones of the Pyramides of Egypt' are nothing but 'the fonde & barbarous ostentation of superfluous riches' (Eden, 1555: A1v). Such was the lineage to which Eden uneasily laid claim, forcing Martyr's colonially ambivalent text into unaccustomed shapes in order to do so (see Hadfield, 1998: 86–9).

Unlike his earlier examples in stone, Eden's book was a living, textual monument in paper: simultaneously elegiac, admonitory, and didactic. In its form and in the deeds it related, he argued, it superseded the classical achievements of Greece and Rome and its contents were unimpeachably true. These are the documents of 'doers'; those who were 'parte of such thynges as are conteyned in the hystorie', whose 'painefull' deeds (Eden, 1555: A2v) are verifiable thanks to a Spanish institution that ensured their memorialisation in a classical sense, but also epistemologically produced their truth: the Casa de la Contratació de las Indias in Seville. Knowledge of this institution was readily available in England thanks to the significant community of English traders in the city and their extensive interactions with it (Dalton, 2016: 41–2). Eden marvels that these Spanish voyagers have 'not onely subdued these landes and seas' but they have 'also with lyke diligence commytted thorder therof to wrytinge' (Eden, 1555: A2v). Conquest is recapitulated – made real – through text. Eden immediately repeats the correlative conjunction to communicate the wonder of this process:

> And not this onely, but for the better tryall of the trewth herein, have and yet doo in maner dayly sende from thense into Spayne such monumentes as are most certeyne testimonies of theyr doynge, as you may reade in dyvers places in this boke. This newe worlde is now so much frequented, the Ocean nowe so well knowen, and the commodities so greate, that the kynge erected a house in the citie of Sivile (cauled the house of the contractes of India) perteyninge onely to thaffayres of the Ocean. (Eden, 1555: A2v)

Eden's point culminates here with a provocatively contradictory pun on 'monuments': both the materially substantial commemoration of great figures in antiquity he celebrates in the opening of his preface, but also a written document or legal record (*Oxford English Dictionary n.* 3a). The illusory permanence of ancient stone gives way to the perpetuity of paper as an increasingly familiar new world necessitated newly bureaucratic methodologies. In this way Eden lays out what he felt the English should aspire to as well as the intellectual foundations of his own textual project. It was much more than what Andrew Fitzmaurice has described as 'an opportunity for his humanistically educated readers to pursue the *vita activa*' (Fitzmaurice, 2003: 35). This was a humanistic fantasy of a whole different order, with Eden exhorting his readers to marvel at the prospect of a working documentary colonialism; at a global Christian empire with an archive at its heart.

Eden's recognition of the potency of voyage accounts for establishing and sustaining an imperium of 'facts' justifies his book and was to have a profound influence in England. It has also shaped Eden's own critical reception: Boies Penrose, for instance, represents a broad seam of scholarship on Eden when he writes that 'the outstanding accomplishment of this book was to present in England a substantial corpus of information on the great discoveries, revealing at the same time the major writers on the subject' (Penrose, 1955: 314). It is a position Eden would surely have been comfortable with, just as he would likely have welcomed Penrose's rather extravagant final assertion that it was only 'with the publication of Eden's *Decades*' that 'we may say that England fully awoke to the new dawn' (Penrose, 1955: 314), even if it does gloss over the intense activity of the previous decade. Yet to characterise Eden (or indeed Hakluyt thirty-four years later) as an inert and objective collector and translator of 'new world' texts is to underestimate his shaping influence on the English *Decades* and the multidirectional interests embedded in it. Editing is here a kind of authorship, with Eden trimming and splicing texts together, occasionally adding his own digressions, and creating something quite distinct from Martyr's original text. This process is particularly pronounced in the two English voyages to West Africa that he includes at the end of the volume.

Penrose is right to highlight the book's importance as a 'corpus', for Eden certainly intended it to play a foundational role in the establishment of an archive of English expansionism. He also wanted it to have efficacy; the latter part of the volume's full title speaks to both professional and lay constituencies in claiming that 'the diligent reader' would be able to 'learne many secreates touchynge the lande, the sea, and the starres, very necessarie to be knowe[n] to al such as shal attempte any navigations, or otherwise have delite to beholde the strange and woonderfull woorkes of God and nature' (Eden, 1555: title page). To that end Eden included some unusual material: following substantial initial sections from Martyr's first three decades, Oviedo, and Pigafetta, he introduces a chapter on 'the prices of precious stones and Spices, with theyr weightes and measures as they are accustomed to bee soulde bothe of the Moores and the gentyles: And of the places where they growe', which is justified, perhaps with a critical edge, 'that wee may not utterly bee ignorant of the thinges which we so greately esteeme and bye so deare' (Eden, 1555: 233v). Subsequent sections include discourses on weights, a series of texts on the Indies, Vespucci on navigating the southern seas, the Muscovy material, Cabot's voyages and information on northern lands, a discussion of Tatars, Gómara on the Indies, more navigational material, the opening chapters of Vannoccio Biringuccio's book on metals, the English African voyages, and Gemma Frisius on longitude.

Throughout this apparently random selection geography and utility remain the presiding themes, with Eden sparring with Pliny and Ptolemy whilst explaining and rationalising at ever greater length as readers work their way through the volume. His is a kind of imperial handbook, an intrinsically connected history in which new and old worlds are made to pivot around the point Eden saw as England's foremost opportunity: the far north-west. In the preface to his earlier *Treatyse* (1553), Eden had similarly vouched that 'it were worthy the adve[n]ture to attempt' the 'stayght called *Fretu[m] trium fratrum*, westward & by North from England, which viage is sufficiently knowen to suche as have any skyll in Geographie' (Eden, 1553: A1v). He goes on to refer to parts of the western world 'where the Eagle (yet not in every place) hath so spred his winges', allowing 'other poor byrdes' to 'without offence seke theyr preye within the compasse of the same'. However he cryptically insists that he 'wyll speak nothing hereof, bycause I wold be loth to lay an egge, wherof other men may hatch a serpent' (Eden, 1553: A2r). Even here, in a book dedicated to Northumberland, Eden was tentative when navigating the Holy Roman Emperor's imperial claims. Two years later, with the publication of the *Decades*, the political and religious circumstances in which he found himself had twisted his recognition of the complexities of English overseas ambition into a personal paranoia generated by the inevitable sensitivities surrounding his advocacy of English imperial prospects under Mary I's Hapsburg-oriented regime. Late in the preface to that work he is much more explicit and, writing of North America, he notes that,

> there yet remayneth an other portion of that mayne lande [the North American continent] reachynge towarde the northeast, thought to be as large as the other, and not yet knowen but only by the sea coastes, neyther inhabyted by any Christian men: whereas neverthelesse (as wryteth Gemma Phrisius) in this lande there are many fayre and frutefull regions, hygh mountaynes, and fayre ryvers, with abundaunce of golde and dyvers kyndes of beastes. Also cities and towres so wel buylded and people of such civilitie, that this parte of the worlde seemeth lyttle inferiour to owre Europe, if thinhabitauntes had receaved owre religion. (Eden, 1555: C1v)

Here Eden is homogenising a vast geographical expanse – the entire eastern seaboard of North America, from 'Terra Florida' in the south to 'Regio Baccalearum or Bacchallaos' (probably Labrador) in the north – for his own propagandist purposes.[8] The fervour with which he presses his case would

---

[8] As Eden acknowledges, he draws the term 'Baccalearum Regio' from Frisius, who on his globe of 1536 depicts a north-western passage between 'Terra Corterealis' and 'Baccalearum Regio'. The

reverberate through John Dee's own elaborate justification for English colonial rights in the far north (on this see Sherman, 1995: 187–200) and in Humphrey Gilbert's *Discourse of a Discoverie for a New Passage to Cataia* (written *c.*1566 but not published until 1576), with Gilbert lifting whole sections of Eden's work for his own northward expansionist proposals.[9] The influence of this same passage can also be traced in the extensive notes provided to Martin Frobisher and his crews by Richard Hakluyt on their search for the North-West Passage. Hakluyt had instructed them on how to proceed if they came across 'the soyle and clymate' of Bordeaux, Portugal, 'the South part of *Spaine* or *Barbarie*' (Hakluyt, 1600: 46). The English crews' experience of Greenland and Baffin was, needless to say, quite different from Eden's confident projections.

His evident enthusiasm for English colonial adventures in the north-west as well as the north-east makes it all the more intriguing that the only contemporary English accounts he includes do not relate western or northern voyages and are not concerned with colonial settlement. This again may reflect his anxious recognition of Spanish imperial dominance, for the concern of both accounts was West Africa, where English merchants were attempting to inveigle themselves into what was considered, post-Tordesillas, as within the Portuguese sphere of imperial ambition (see Hair, 1994). For David Gwyn these accounts appealed to Eden for precisely this reason: they and the wider volume offered 'proof' of his 'loyalty to the new regime at a time when others had chosen rebellion', events darkly referenced in Eden's preface. Furthermore 'it was an adroit move, combining praise for the Spanish people and their rulers with the clear hint to the court that England's future lay in encouraging trade' (Gwyn, 1984: 29). The contemporaneity of the events these accounts relate also had an obvious appeal, with the return of the second voyage preceding publication by only a few months.

Eden's justification for their inclusion is detailed and substantial. He initially explains that because 'the parteners at whose charge this book is prynted wolde long since have ne proceeded no further' he had 'not thought to have written any thynge of these voyages', a remark which hints at some disquiet among the printers at the book's idiosyncrasies. However, 'the liberalitie of master Toy [Richard Toy, one of the printers involved] encouraged me to attempt the same' (Eden, 1555: 360v). In his preface to the accounts he elaborates: at the last minute he 'was desyred by certeyne my freindes to

---

Labrador region was often named Bacalaos, or variants of it, after the Portuguese, Spanish, and Breton word for cod.

[9] For example, Eden's extensive reliance on Pliny in arguing for the existence of a north-east passage, and specifically his use of Cornelius Nepos.

make summe mention of these viages' (Eden, 1555: 343v). In keeping with Eden's repeated return to the necessity of textual memory for voyages of conquest and exploration he suggests that their printing would enable 'sum memorie therof' to,

> remayne to owr posteritie if eyther iniquitie of tyme consumynge all thinges, or ignoraunce creepynge in by barbarousnesse and contempt of knowledge, shulde hereafter bury in oblivion so woorthy attemptes, so much the greatlyer to bee esteemed as before never enterprysed by Englysshe men.
>
> (Eden, 1555: 343v)

If English commercial initiative was to be stifled or swallowed up by virtue of its subservient position within a wider Spanish imperium, this passage appears to suggest, then these brief records would at least remain as a memorial to English enterprise and what might have resulted from the mid-century expansionist policies in which he had been so closely involved. Alternatively, if Eden's instincts were right, and gaps within the Spanish-Portuguese division of the world remained to be exploited, then these two accounts might represent the first documents of the English expansionary archive he so fervently advocated.

Eden then immediately embarks upon a short and furious attack on the current papally endorsed status quo. He hopes English merchants will be able to pursue the opportunity these West African excursions represent. But they will only be able to do so,

> if the same be not hyndered by thambision of such as for the conquestynge of fortie or fyftie myles here and there, and erectynge of certayne fortresses or rather blockhouses amonge naked people, think the[m] selves woorthy to bee lordes of halfe the worlde, envying that other shulde enjoy the commodities which they them selves can not holy possesse. (Eden, 1555: 343v)

With a curious and provocatively contradictory echo of his initial celebration of the 'mercyfull' Spanish conquests of 'these naked peoples' of the Americas (in which a 'greater commoditie hath therof ensewed to the vanquisshed then to the victourers') Eden excoriates Portuguese pretensions to govern half the globe (Eden, 1555: A2v).[10] With this further, bitter reflection on the Iberian carving up of the world with papal sanction in the Treaties of Alcaçòvas (1479), Tordesillas (1494), and Zaragoza (1529) – a running theme – Eden suggests such pretensions are unjust and illusory. For a volume that opens with an apparent endorsement of Spanish imperial greatness, the language of this attack undercuts the

---

[10] Eden's use of 'naked' in this passage is actually the third example in his text: the second is a marginal gloss that Hadfield similarly identifies as a contradiction of the first usage and an attack on Spanish colonial practices (Hadfield, 1998: 88).

whole enterprise and its lofty claims to pre-eminence in almost Swiftian terms.[11]

More immediately Eden's anti-Portuguese diatribe resonates with another document to which it appears to be closely connected. Early in 1555 João III had despatched the ambassador Lopes de Sousa from the Portuguese court to formally protest at English infringements in Guinea. He was to demand 'reparations for damage, restoration of merchandise, punishment of offenders and a veto on all further Guinea operations' (Andrews, 1984: 107–8) where, as Giovanni Michieli, the Venetian ambassador, reported, the Portuguese king 'pretends that it is all his and under his jurisdiction' (quoted in Blake, 1942: II. 354). The intervention was not immediately successful, probably thanks to Privy Council support for the merchants' cause. At some point in mid 1555 those involved responded formally to the Portuguese allegations with a petition (perhaps drafted with Eden's input) that makes precisely the same argument as Eden's introduction. We, the English merchants asserted, do 'by the common usage of the worlde' use 'traficque in all places of the worlde as well Asia and Africa as Europa'. According to 'this our accustomed usage, we have of late resorted to sundry places, both to the south and the north parties of the world, in both which we finde the governors and the people of the places well willing to receive us frindly and jentely' (SP 69/7 no. 449, quoted in Blake, 1942: II. 355– 6). This quiet traffic, 'exchauncing merchandises for merchandises', they argued, was undertaken with the necessary Indigenous sanction and outside Portuguese jurisdictions. Indeed, 'our factors landed not in anie place where the said king [of Portugal] had anie fortresse, towne, garrison or governaunce or anie officer or other person, that did forbidd them' and those factors properly 'refused to use any traficque untill they wer infourmed' by the people 'that they wer no subjectes to the King of Portugall' (Blake, 1942: II. 356).

English enterprise in the north and south is again explicitly linked; ancient commercial rights and practices common to all are implicitly privileged over unsustainable territorial claims; and, perhaps more importantly, something approximating an Indigenous right to self-determination overrides vague, expansive imperial assertions. In this the English merchants (perhaps intentionally) failed to grasp the model of fortress-enforced monopolising that had proven so effective for the Portuguese in West Africa and Southeast Asia (Thornton, 1998: 59–63). Instead they clung to an older model of empire more akin to the Spanish approach: if the Portuguese could not control the regions they claimed to rule – if they were not recognised as the legitimate overlords

---

[11] As can be found in the savage anti-colonial attack of the final chapter of *Gulliver's Travels* (1726), on which more later in this Element.

by their supposedly subject populations – then their claimed authority was a fiction and they could not legitimately proscribe the trading rights of other European nations. This argument is clearly at work in the merchants' assertion that 'the said inhabitauntes of that country offred us and our said factors ground to builde uppon, if they would make anie fortresses in their countrey, and further offred them assistaunce of certen slaves for those workes without anie charge'. It is also affirmed in the efforts the English factors undertook to obtain the licence of 'the King of Byne [Benin]' without which 'they might neither buye nor sell', enabling them to traffic 'frely and liberally' (Blake, 1942: II. 357). The English merchants signed off on a plaintive note: they had undertaken this trade 'without malice, moved by the common fredome of all merchauntes' and had endeavoured to obey 'all commaundementes' imposed upon them as a result of Portuguese sensitivities. They pointed to unrestrained French commercial ventures along the same African coasts and regretted that 'occupieng merchandizes shold be so discoraged' with English merchants 'more restreyned or bo[u]nd then other merchauntes of strange countries be' (Blake, 1942: II. 358).

Eden's decision to include these first English voyage accounts was therefore not motivated primarily by considerations of posterity, as he had argued. If Gwyn's calculation that the book was put on sale in September 1555 and 'many copies were published' (Gwyn, 1984: 30) is correct, then it appeared just at the right moment to play a decisive role in the Anglo-Portuguese dispute, which was not resolved until December of that year. These first English accounts were therefore included as part of a determined and remarkable two-pronged effort in print and formal petition to assert English mercantile rights to the Guinea coast and a fundamental set of commercial principles that underpinned those rights. They were mobilised as part of a wider struggle to maintain an Edwardian policy of commercial expansion (clearly referenced in the 1555 petition) and an attempt to counter Spanish and, most prominently, Portuguese attempts to suppress it through their greater influence on the crown.

As an immediate propagandist exercise Eden's efforts failed completely. On 16 December 1555, the Venetian ambassador Michieli wrote back to the Doge and Senate that the Portuguese ambassador 'has obtained the settlement desired by him with regard to his affair concerning the Guinea navigation'. On 'hearing King Philip's opinion' Queen Mary 'gave orders for the vessels destined for that voyage' to be 'disarmed and unloaded, much to the regret of those Londoners, who are concerned in this navigation, as they thus lose the opportunity for making great profits, in accordance with the experiment made by them' (Blake, 1942: II. 354). All 'Marchaunts that occupye to Gynney' had already been called before the Lord Mayor of London to receive royal instructions 'to staie from further trafique in those partes' (PC 2/7, 1555, f.283r). On 30 December, the Privy Council then issued compensation for the losses of those merchants directly involved. It must have been scant consolation, for the Venetian reference to King Philip confirmed Eden's fears: it had now become 'Spain's policy to support the Portuguese empire against intruders, for French oceanic aggression threatened the Iberian powers equally and English expansion was now beginning to take the same course' (Andrews, 1984: 108). The English seaborne ventures recorded for the first time and wholeheartedly endorsed by Eden were now prohibited as a threat to an apparently unchallengeable Iberian world order.

A febrile environment, a palpable sense of betrayal, and a host of competing political forces therefore pulled and twisted Eden's book into its final shape, justifying and generating the Guinea material. All of this invariably left an imprint on the narratives themselves, often in unexpected and contradictory ways. This is sometimes identified as a fault in Eden. His role in producing these texts has often either been overlooked or critiqued by historians of the period and, in contrast to those who followed him, he is not widely known: even Hakluyt, who drew on his work repeatedly, chose not to include Eden in his list of '*writers of Geographie*' alongside Adams and Ramusio (Hakluyt, 1582: 1v). John W. Blake – whose important work is used extensively by Andrews and others – is crushingly scrupulous in identifying the many 'defects' in Eden's reproduction of the Guinea material, with some justification. For Blake, Eden is 'credulous, imaginative, unscientific, and very much influenced by classical and biblical tradition' (Blake, 1942: II. 255). He exceeds even 'the usual defects of his age', is 'uncritical' and unable 'to sort out the reliable from the doubtful' (Blake, 1942: II. 256), and, perhaps most damningly, he is too prone to 'additions and embellishments' (Blake, 1942: II. 257). Hair and Alsop found that Eden put together these texts 'hastily and clumsily' (Hair and Alsop, 1992: 1). In a similar vein David Olusoga has described Eden's book as 'dubious' (Olusoga, 2016: 53). Of course many of the same accusations can be made of the English voyage writing that followed, and this is the point. Eden's work on the two Guinea narratives, one quite different from the other, sketches out the forms in which this material would, even could be published in England for decades to follow. Most of these points are indisputable – these texts *are* disordered and contradictory – but I am interested in holding Eden's work up to slightly different scrutiny: to ask how and why this material appears the way that it does, and in the process reflect on how a mid-sixteenth-century compiler of travel material like Eden assembled his accounts and the paper empires those accounts in turn were constituting. Any understanding of how Eden 'produced' these particular voyage narratives – texts that he did not exactly write himself – can only come from their close reading.

2 Gold: The First Guinea Voyage

High summer in 1553 brought with it confusion and jeopardy across England. The boy-king Edward VI had died on 6 July and in his final illness had conspired with Northumberland in an attempt to fix a Protestant succession by excluding his sisters Mary and Elizabeth and resolving upon Jane Grey. Once Mary publicly resolved to contest her right to the crown English subjects and organisations had to reflect on where their own allegiances lay whilst calculating the likely outcome. It was a delicate moment in which confessional and political as well as dynastic futures hung in the balance.

In Portsmouth, at this point a small port town with only a few thousand inhabitants, the situation was particularly difficult. In the harbour lay a fleet of three ships – the *Lion*, the *Primrose*, and a pinnace, the *Moon* – crewed, victualled, and ready to sail for Guinea under the command of Thomas Wyndham. Theirs was another speculative initiative that had developed out of the commercially expansionist strategies pressed by Northumberland in which Wyndham had been closely involved. However, this small fleet's departure was stayed as the drama of succession was played out, at least in part because of Marian suspicions concerning the purpose of the voyage and of the allegiance of its admiral. Delay represented potential catastrophe for the investors, who included a sequence of powerful London grandees, men such as Sir George Barne, Sir John Yorke, Sir William Garrard, and Francis Lambert, many of whom must have feared the loss of more than simply their funds and ships: a Marian succession had profound implications for English foreign policy and would likely curtail this short-lived period of English commercial endeavour (Andrews, 1984: 104). From commander to investors these men were also Protestants: indeed their investments, ambitions, and faith were closely bound together.

For Mary and her advisors Wyndham and his ships were a potential problem. An experienced soldier and seaman, Wyndham had seen distinguished service in Ireland in 1539–40 and had captained ships and troops during the 'Rough Wooing' campaign against Scotland between 1544 and 1548. His success is reflected in high office: he was made Master of Naval Ordnance and Vice-Admiral of the English fleet in 1547, but he was also often associated with piracy (Alsop, 2004). Wyndham's portrait was painted by Hans Eworth around 1550 and depicts a bluff and brusque figure. His military accoutrements – the helmet to his right, the musket slung across his back, and the powder flask hung around his neck – all signal his confident dominance of the Arcadian realm behind him (which itself features a tented military camp to the fore) that likely represents Ireland but might equally reflect his campaigns in Scotland (see

Figure 1). The implicit violence anticipates his later methods in West Africa. Under the Edwardian regime Wyndham was drawn into Northumberland's new vision for English expansion and became a captain and part owner of the *Lion* of London, in which he spearheaded attempts to establish a direct trade with Morocco. His two voyages proved lucrative, exchanging cargoes of linen, woollens, coral, and amber for North African sugar, molasses, dates and almonds in Safi and Santa Cruz de Aguer, Agadir. Navigating overlapping Portuguese, Moroccan, and Spanish spheres of dominance, this was precisely the type of para-imperial initiative, underpinned by increasingly flexible English commercial/financial structures and backed up with political support, that Northumberland, Eden and others in Edward VI's court saw as the key to England's future prosperity (Dimmock, 2019: 7–8).

Wyndham was therefore a prominent representative of a foreign policy antagonistic to Spanish and Portuguese imperial and commercial interests. He

Figure 1 Hans Eworth, *Portrait of Thomas Wyndham*, *c*.1550. Longford Castle

was also politically suspect. Having served alongside Northumberland in the Scottish campaigns of the 1540s, he was already connected to the man who became de facto regent from 1550 and they were closely associated through the navy. Northumberland had been Vice-Admiral and then Admiral of the Royal Navy for a more than a decade from 1537, at the same time Wyndham was building a reputation as a naval commander. One of Northumberland's closest supporters, Sir Thomas, Lord Darcy of Chiche, was Wyndham's half-brother (an investor in the Iceland fishery, Darcy was also a prominent founding member of the Muscovy Company: Willan, 1953: 10–11, 90). All of this was enough to generate fears that the fleet at anchor in Portsmouth in early July 1553 might be used to secure the Grey succession and/or could antagonise Mary's Roman Catholic allies in Europe. In the event, Northumberland's plans for the succession unravelled quickly: he was in prison by 19 July and the new Privy Council declared itself loyal to Mary. Wyndham and others were summoned to London on 25 July, presumably to explain the fleet's purpose (two of its ships were leased from the crown) and to profess their loyalty (Alsop, 2004). He was given permission to depart five days later and the fleet finally left Portsmouth for West Africa on 12 August, only ten days before Northumberland was executed for treason.

So Wyndham left England in deeply unsettled circumstances and could not have been sure of the political climate to which he would return. In response he seems to have resolved that profit was the only sure route to domestic glory and the restitution of his reputation, and that meant gold. The west coast of Africa, from modern-day Senegal to Nigeria – much of which, for European observers, was covered by the term 'Guinea' – had become particularly associated with gold in the Christian European imagination. Slavery, whether orchestrated by the Portuguese, Dutch, French, or English, came to this region much later (Shumway, 2011a: 33). To assume it was the dominant European interest is to underplay West Africa's flourishing trade networks and major importance as a supplier of gold and other products to European markets: as Richard Bean has pointed out, in this part of West Africa 'the export of cotton cloth, wax, hides, wood, gum, pepper, ivory, and most especially gold, were together much more important in terms of value than were slaves for quite some time' (Bean, 1974: 351). It was the wealth of this trade and its multifaceted interconnection with European markets (see Ebert, 2008: 53–78) that drew in English, French, and later Dutch attempts to circumvent or outmuscle the monopoly claimed by the Portuguese in the region.

Importantly, these were late medieval and early modern developments. Africa and gold were not associated in classical literature: Lucan stated that no gold was mined in Africa, and neither 'Strabo nor Pliny mention Africa as a source of gold' (Garrard, 1982: 446). It is only by the early sixteenth century that English printed texts began to make vague assertions of 'Ethiopian' riches, with the term 'Ethiopian' referring to the all peoples south of Egypt and the Maghreb. As Eden noted in the 'breefe description of Affrike' with which he prefaced the Wyndham account, south of those regions 'is the kyngedome of Guinea, with Senga, Iaiofo, Gambra, and manye other regions of the blacke Moores cauled Ethiopians or Negros' (Eden, 1555: 344r). Coastal, riverine, and caravan routes had encouraged the development of a complex internal trade over centuries, enabling West African ivory, pepper, gold, and slaves to reach Mediterranean markets across the Sahara and European cloth, swords, and paper to travel in the reverse direction (Brooks, 2018: 49). Information on the jealously guarded and lucrative Portuguese trade in the region began to reach English attention from early on, at least from the mid fifteenth century, facilitated by the close relations between the two countries (Hair and Alsop, 1992: 5; Dalton, 2016: 23–4). It was not until a flurry of interest registered in London's printing presses a century later, however, that any detailed information began to be circulated in print, and was first referenced in any detail in Eden's own *Treatyse* (1553) and in William Prat's translation of Boemus, *The discription of the contrey of Aphrique* (1554). Similarly, Eden's foregrounding of gold in his account is in keeping with its prominence in the *Decades* as a whole: as might be expected in a text concerned with opening up the world to its readers, it is absolutely obsessed with the metal. This was, after all, 'one of the great themes of the fifteenth and sixteenth centuries' although it remained more readily associated with the Americas than Africa at this point (Greenblatt, 1991: 64). Eden includes a history of the gold trade and gold mining and characterises Spanish imperial glory in part through its vast acquisition of gold (whilst registering proper Christian disapproval). He even gives his reader the 'Indian' word for gold: 'cauni' (Eden, 1555: b4r).

Gold was therefore on Wyndham's mind and for his financial backers this was a new trade and a major opportunity. Eden registers this explicitly in his text, calling this first expedition a 'golden vyage' (Eden, 1555: 345v) and later following Portuguese precedent in referring to the coasts of Elmina ('Mina') as 'the golden lande' (Eden, 1555: 346r). Wyndham also had a specific advantage in accessing those markets. Travelling with him were two renegade Portuguese who had considerable experience in the region, Antonio Anes Pinteado and Francisco Rodrigues, who had lost favour in the Portuguese court and sought patronage in England. Despite frenzied attempts by the Portuguese to coax or abduct them home and to prevent the voyage altogether, Pinteado – 'one of the foremost commanders in Atlantic trade and naval operations' (Andrews, 1984: 106) – became Wyndham's 'petycaptaine' or vice-admiral and Rodrigues became his pilot. The Portuguese contribution was therefore profoundly important, so much so that Christopher Ebert has cautioned against taking Eden and Hakluyt too literally in fashioning these as 'English' voyages when from a different perspective they represent renegade Portuguese factions baulking at the restraints placed upon them by their own crown's monopoly (Ebert, 2008: 53–8). It is certainly the case that the Portuguese presence on this and later voyages complicates their narration as well as their nationalism, as we will see shortly. Wyndham also managed to acquire a French surgeon ('Guillam John') with experience of the common diseases of the region (Blake, 1942: II. 282; Hair and Alsop, 1992: 8). After skirmishing with the Portuguese in the Madeiras this multinational crew arrived at the River Nuon or Nipoué, known to the Portuguese as the 'Cestos' (which now forms part of the border between Liberia and Côte d'Ivoire). There they traded on the Mane fringes of the declining Songhai Empire, accumulating a cargo of Malagueta pepper (*Aframomum melegueta*), often identified as grains of paradise, whereupon Pinteado urged a homeward course but, characteristically, the 'tragicall' and 'untame' Wyndham would not listen (Eden, 1555: 346r, 346v).

The fleet plundered on to the Elmina coast of present-day Ghana, attacking Portuguese shipping whilst avoiding the Portuguese fort of São Jorge and, interpolating themselves directly into the long-established trade of the Fante merchants in the region, acquired 150 pounds of gold. Although it was now late in the season and, despite Pinteado's repeated pleas, Wyndham insisted on pressing on a further 150 leagues to Benin. Anchoring in the River Benin he sent Pinteado, Rodrigues, and a number of English merchants upriver via Ughoton to the court of the Oba of Benin, almost certainly in Benin City (although it is not named in the account). At this point, under Oba Orhogbua (reigned 1550–78: see Figure 2), the Benin Empire had reached its greatest extent and the English representatives were received with pomp and ceremony that clearly left a strong impression upon them.

This king was 'a blacke moore (although not so blacke as the rest)' and 'sat in a great houge haule longe and wyde, the walles made of earthe withowte windowes, the roofe of thynne boordes open in sundry places' (Eden, 1555: 346v–347r). In a remark typical of English observers when confronted with order and religiosity elsewhere, the Oba's people give him reverence 'such that if wee wolde gyve as much to owr saviour Chryst, we shuld remove from owr heades many plages which wee dayly deserve for owre contempte and impietie' (Eden, 1555: 347r). This same reverence is captured in a contemporary Beninean brass plaque which depicts Orhogbua carrying his staff of office and surrounded by divine symbolism, adorned with *iwu*, or royal tattoos, and wearing a heavily embroidered wrapper, all contributing to the awesome visual

99.225

Figure 2 Bronze plaque depicting Oba Orhogbua, late sixteenth century.
Horniman Museum 99.225 © Horniman Museum and Gardens

spectacle of his power: as the English noted, 'when his noble men are in his presence, they never looke hym in the face, but syt courynge ... not lookynge uppe untyll the kynge commaunde them' (Eden, 1555: 347r).

Obtaining licence and safe conduct directly from the Oba was a major achievement for the English merchants, as reflected in their brandishing of it in response to subsequent Portuguese objections (see Ryder, 1969: 76–8). This sanction enabled Pinteado and the others to acquire a further 'foure score toonne' of pepper (Eden, 1555: 347v). Meanwhile, however, catastrophe was engulfing the fleet: as Pinteado had warned, a sickness consisting of 'swellynges and agues' had broken out and ravaged the company, ultimately killing both Wyndham and Pinteado himself (Eden, 1555: 347v). In the desperate scramble to get back to England one ship – the privately owned *Lion* in which Wyndham had a share – was abandoned and English merchants were left behind at the Benin court. Of the one hundred and forty who sailed from England, many of them West Country mariners who had been pressed into service, barely forty arrived back in Plymouth in June 1554. With many fewer sailors to pay, this brutal toll was of course a boon to the investors, for whom 'it proved a highly profitable venture' (Andrews, 1984: 107). Such profits quickly generated a second, less eventful voyage, led by John Lok and financed again by Barne, Yorke, Thomas Lok (brother of John), and others. They had learned the lessons of Wyndham's folly and returned to the River Nuon/Nipoué (which the English called 'Sestos') for pepper and to the Elmina coast of Ghana for gold and ivory. Lok's voyage again turned a considerable profit, and he lost only twenty-four of his crew (the account of which is discussed in more detail in the next section). The two voyages had enabled the compiling of detailed intelligence on the commercial possibilities of the West African region, especially concerning those English items that were considered saleable: such information, simultaneously being assembled for as many regions of the globe as possible, was, as Eden acknowledges, worth more than the gold with which they had returned. The Portuguese certainly recognised this. It was the efficient success of Lok's enterprise in particular that generated the Portuguese protests to which Eden responded so vehemently.

That Eden chose to incorporate accounts of both these voyages in his new book is remarkable, not solely because of their urgent contemporaneity. As I have suggested already, they usefully represented in practice an English mercantile strategy that he had advocated from the start. Nor was it remarkable solely because of his open acknowledgement of the pressure exerted upon him to include them by 'certayne my frendes' (Eden, 1555: 343v) which bound him into an orchestrated attempt to thwart Portuguese efforts to stifle this new and promising trade. Rather, their appearance is surprising because the Wyndham account in particular resists any easy incorporation into a valorisation of English overseas endeavours. That narrative appears to contradict almost everything I have so far highlighted in Eden's furious framing of them both – his idealisation of the honest pursuit of glory and profit – and it is a dissonance in which Eden is fulsomely complicit. The account of the Wyndham voyage is the more striking example of the two, for it reads like a prolonged character assassination in which the English Wyndham's folly and rapacity are blamed for each of the fleet's miscalculations and its ultimate fate, and are repeatedly contrasted with the wronged and righteous (and Portuguese) Pinteado, a 'wyse, discrete, and sober man' (Eden, 1555: 345v) who, in the short space of the outward journey, became 'as a man tormented with the company of a terrible hydra' (Eden, 1555: 346r).

From the very opening of the narrative Eden does not hesitate to lambast the English captain: in this voyage Pinteado had been, he writes,

> evyll matched with an unequall coompanion and unlyke matche of most sundry qualities and conditions with vertues few or none adourned, with vices dyvers and many fowly spotted, knowen of many with out profyte, and desyred of fewe or none for his wyckednes: whose smaule acquayntaunce was profitable to all men, and his familiar conversation an undoinge, that happye was the man or woman that knewe hym not, he for his gooddes and shee for her name. (Eden, 1555: 345v)

Everything about this passage is excessive: Wyndham's supposed vices quickly swell to imply absolute moral corruption. This was too much for later editors of the account: in Richard Willes's *The History of Travayle* it is cut, likely because it was deemed unnecessarily incendiary, and Richard Hakluyt followed Willes in both editions of *The Principal Navigations* (Willes, 1577: 338v; Hakluyt, 1589: 85). Later in the text readers are even given reported speech for a flavour of Wyndham's violent raging, for in 'revilynge the sayde Pinteado, caulynge hym Jewe with other opprobrious woordes', he exclaimed to his crew: 'This horson Jewe hath promised to brynge us to such places as are not, or as he can not bring us unto. But if he doo not, I wyl cut of his eares and naile them to the mast' (Eden, 1555: 346v). The second Guinea account, relating Lok's voyage, is almost the opposite: its technical details of navigation and topography are so dry that Eden repeatedly steps in to add narrative colour and proto-anthropological interest. Indeed it may not be accurate to describe them as two distinct accounts at all, for Eden treats them as one extended, ambivalent reflection on this new Guinea trade and its establishment in which the Wyndham voyage provides 'the hystory' and the Lok voyage 'the course of the navigation' (Eden, 1555: 349v). The second thus augments the first in order to offer practical advice for those seeking to further prosecute the trade.

Some of this apparent contradiction can be explained by sources and circumstance. It may be (as Blake suggests) that Eden only had access to a deeply partial narrative of the first voyage produced by Pinteado's allies (possibly the pilot Rodrigues, who 'may well have been the informant on Benin customs for Eden's account – if he survived the return voyage': Hair and Alsop, 1992: 8) and not those he could have sourced from Wyndham's followers, which the account makes clear were in the majority. The tone and focus of the narrative may well reflect the bitterness and grief of those merchant investors whose factors and family members had been abandoned or lost, something Eden hints at a number of points in the text (Hair and Alsop, 1992: 10–11; see Eden, 1555: 345v). Furthermore, it is certainly possible that Wyndham, a distinguished naval officer in royal service and an experienced soldier with a taste for piracy but also attentive to the well-being of those serving under him (Alsop, 2004), was the unstable, tyrannical monster that Eden portrays. Certainly Andrews and other historians have been persuaded: for him the most remarkable aspect of Wyndham's voyage was 'his aggressive, predatory and brutal conduct of it' (Andrews, 1984: 106). Yet none of these scenarios adequately explain the contradictions in the text. Eden's careful framing of the initial accounts he had solicited or was provided; adding, splicing, foregrounding Wyndham's villainy; his advocacy of an English trade threatened by Portuguese opposition; and the prominence of his own connections to these voyages, either through his 'freindes' in the case of the first, or his own direct interaction with the sailors and merchandise of the second voyage, all indicate that he shaped these narratives with a particular intent. Had he wanted to downplay Wyndham's role (or even adopt his version of events) and thereby turn these accounts into simpler triumphs of English commercial daring and ingenuity, he could certainly have done so. Why did he choose not to?

The same question certainly occurred to the anonymous editor of the late seventeenth-century anthology *The Golden coast, or, A description of Guinney* (1665) when they came to reproduce the Wyndham voyage as the originary point for what had become an enormously lucrative English enterprise. According to this version, and in direct contravention of Eden's account, 'happy was that man that could go' with the 'sevenscore lusty men' who sailed out from Portsmouth that August (20). It presents a vision of harmony and plenitude that is only briefly punctured by an erroneous note indicating that somewhere between the Madeiras and the Canaries, 'there happening a difference between the two Captains', the 'Marriners cast off one of them' (20). The geography has been improbably mangled in order that the second, Lok voyage could then be stitched together with the first to create a single, lengthy, and suitably successful whole, perhaps reflecting Eden's initial willingness to bind them as generic negatives of each other. Clearly by 1665 it was felt that the Eden narrative of Wyndham's voyage was an unsuitable starting point for such a celebrated trade.

Why Eden chose not to frame his own account in this way can, I want to suggest, be explained by examining the way he necessarily caters for multiple, distinct readerships. These first published Tudor voyage narratives are surprisingly conscious of their readers. Their oddities and the pronounced differences between the two accounts are in this respect a consequence of the challenges generated by this awareness and the nature of the mid-sixteenth-century print marketplace. All writing intended for circulation in the public domain was to some extent created by its audiences, but it simultaneously had to appear the opposite. This was especially important for accounts of travel which, regardless of their fictionality, had always to insist on their own unequivocal truthfulness. In the case of Eden and these particular narratives, reconciling the conflicting expectations of those different constituencies, the more general as well as the courtly or mercantile reader, generated a polyvocal text that nevertheless asserted its own univocality, a deeply partial text that nevertheless proclaimed its own impartial truthfulness and the absolute probity of its editor. This is very much in keeping with the instability of the form I highlighted earlier and is indicative of an undefined and unfixed genre coming into being. The narrative fractures and contortions this creates are evident from the very beginning: Eden assures his readers that 'at this presente it is not my intent to accuse or defend, approve or improve' and accordingly he 'wil cease to speake any further hereof, and proceade to the descriptio[n] of the fyrst viage as briefly and faythfully as I was advertised of the same'. Crucially that information came from 'such credible persons as made diligent inquisition to knowe the truth hereof as much as shalbe requisite' and Eden has only cut out those 'many particular thynges not greatly necessarie to be knowen'. Tellingly he finishes this paragraph with a self-exculpatory and moralistic flourish:

> And if herein favoure or frendshyppe shall perhappes cause sum to thinke that sum have byn sharpely touched, let them laye a parte favoure and frendshippe and gyve place to truth, that honest men may receave prayse for well doinge, and lewde persons reproche as the just stipende of theyr evyll desertes, whereby other may bee deterred to do the lyke, and vertuous men encouraged to proceade in honest attemptes. (Eden, 1555: 343v)

In anticipation of disquiet at the treatment of Wyndham, Eden deftly shifts responsibility away from himself and onto the reader. They need to examine their own partiality before they impugn his, he suggests, and trust that evil will out in the end.

Eden's anxious address thus speaks to all his constituencies at once. To those commercial backers and 'freindes' whose interests he represents through the publication of these accounts, Eden offers a finely calibrated defence of pre-existing mercantile policy and the importance of continuing in 'honest attemptes'. To the crown and court he presents a condemnation of Wyndham that perhaps implicitly damns him for his close association with Northumberland and the previous regime whilst explicitly condemning him for his greed and serial improprieties. In imperilling the royal ships and his crew solely in the pursuit of gold, Wyndham's behaviour demonstrates the fallacy of overstretching English capacity and – in conjunction with the quiet, purposeful accumulation of the second voyage – makes an eloquent case for an English focus on the Guinea pepper trade associated with the coast of modern-day Liberia rather than anything that could be seen to infringe on Portuguese interests too aggressively. Here Eden is engaged in actively refashioning the enterprise to render it viable in accordance with new Marian priorities. As I have already noted, he is also responding directly to the Portuguese: actual hostilities between the English and the Portuguese forces in the Madeiras are carefully excised from Eden's book (Andrews, 1984: 106) and Wyndham's catastrophic folly could in no way confirm Portuguese accusations of aggression, damage, and infringement. In the published version of events, even the unstable Wyndham conducted trade only with Indigenous sanction and did so in a 'frindly and jentely' fashion, according to recognised rules of commercial engagement, and never intended to attack Portuguese possessions, contrary to what 'the kynge of Portugale was sinisterly informed' (Eden, 1555: 345v). Finally, Eden also speaks directly to his educated English readers, less immediately involved in the trade and its controversies. For them he shapes a romance-inflected cautionary tale that is tentatively nationalistic at a point when some feared England's absorption into Spain's imperial orbit, that is prepared to celebrate the defection of high-ranking and experienced Portuguese sailors to the English (and to defend them at length), and that unapologetically vaunts a specific, para-imperial model of mercantile endeavour 'as before never enterprysed by Englysshe men' (Eden, 1555: 343v).

It is for these readers that Eden makes his most substantial and significant interventions. Preceding the first Guinea voyage he includes a 'breefe description of Affrike' in order that 'these vyages may bee more playnely understode of al men' (Eden, 1555: 343v), an ambition only slightly undercut by an immediate digression into longitudinal detail. John W. Blake was surprised to find that in this section Eden did not turn for information on the West Africa interior to 'trustworthy contemporaries, Moors, negroes or Portuguese', but instead drew mainly on 'rumour and the works of classical writers!' (Blake, 1942: II. 253). For him it consequently had little value, containing nothing but 'gross defects' (Blake, 1942: II. 255), even if he does accord Eden the credit of being 'the first Englishman to publish a description of Africa in the vernacular' (Blake, 1942: II. 256), an honour which should properly be accorded Prat's aforementioned translation of Boemus from the previous year (on Prat see Young, 2015: 158–61). Yet Blake's legitimate lament over a prevailing lack of accuracy sidesteps Eden's approach to this material, its currency, and his intent in assembling it. Turning to classical authorities for his geography, he looked primarily to Ptolemy, whose work was still being extensively published and debated by Eden's European contemporaries: the latest edition of *Geographiae Claudii Ptolemaei Alexandrini* by Sebastian Münster (with which Eden was thoroughly familiar) had been published only three years earlier in Basle (Münster, 1552). It is from Ptolemy that the Roman divisions of North Africa ('Mauritania Tingitania, and Cesariensis': Eden, 1555: 344r) come in Eden's description, for instance. Elsewhere, Eden appears to draw upon a yet more contemporary source: the *Delle descrittione dell-Africa* included in Ramusio's 1550 *Delle navigationi e viaggi* written by the celebrated North African traveller, diplomat, and convert al-Hassan ibn Muhammad al-Wazzan al-Fasi, whose papally bestowed Christian name was Joannes Leo Africanus (see Zemon Davis, 2007). This text would later be translated in its entirety by John Pory and published in English as *A geographical historie of* Africa in 1600. Certainly Eden's and al-Wazzan's delineations of the kingdoms of Marrocko, Fes, and Tremisen appear identical (Ramusio, 1550: 1v; Eden, 1555: 344r).

Eden's opening description of Africa ends with an intriguing account of the legendary Prester John. This drove Blake to particular distraction: in this 'most fantastic passage' the 'credulous' Eden had 'let his imagination run riot' (Blake, 1942: II. 255–6). One can understand Blake's frustration: Prester John (or 'Presbyter Johannes') was a legendary figure in the Christian imagination, a lost Christian monarch whose existence promised military relief from the Muslim Ottoman 'Turks', but also the recovery of a preserved, original faith. Although consistently placed in 'the extreme Orient' in the earliest accounts, such as in the mid-twelfth-century letter of Bishop Hugh of Jabala (Silverberg, 1996: 6–7), in later accounts Prester John was relocated to Africa and became elided with Ethiopian monarchs during the period of their imperial expansion, and with Coptic Christianity. In Eden's account Prester John is 'well knowen to the Portugales in theyr vyages to Calicut' and governs vast dominions encompassing 'many other kynges both Chrystian and hethen that pay hym trybute' (Eden, 1555: 344v). There is contemporary detail – the Portuguese are said to send him 'yearely .viii. shyppes laden with marchaundies' – but older motifs also resurface: were his realms not contained by mountains and 'greate desertes of a hundreth dayes jorney' then this 'Chrystian Emperour' would already 'have invaded the kyngedome of Egypt and the citie of Alcayer [Cairo]', which had been absorbed into the Ottoman Empire with Selim I's victorious campaign over the Mamluk sultanate in 1516–17 (Eden, 1555: 345r).

None of this is the product of Eden's imagination, however. The entire passage is taken and translated virtually word for word from another collection of voyages, Antonio Manuzio's *Viaggi fatti da Venetia alla Tana in Persia*, published in Venice only a decade earlier, and specifically from Luigi Roncinotto's account of his travels in Ethiopia that had begun in 1532 (Manuzio, 1543: 98–9). No doubt a crucial element of its appeal to Eden, the eyewitness basis of Roncinotto's narrative explains why its emphasis falls less on the legendary and more on the contemporary, in the process finding a reassuring continuity between the two (for more on Roncinotto, see Casale, 2010: 49). Hence the unequivocal identification between the mythic Prester John and the 'myghty prince' who 'is cauled David Themperour of Ethiopia' (Eden, 1555: 344v). This was Lebna Dengel, whose regnal name was Dāwīt (or David) II, ruler of Ethiopia from 1508 to 1540. Dengel had sent widely celebrated letters via emissaries to both Manuel I and João III of Portugal proposing joint military operations in the Red Sea and sought Christian allies to counteract the growing dominance of the Ottomans in the region (Salvadore, 2010: 622). This was certainly in keeping with a prevailing anti-Ottomanism elsewhere in Eden's text: once English attempts on the North-East Passage to Cathay proved successful, he wrote, 'the great Cham of Cathay and the Shah of Persia on the one side, and the Christian princes on the other side, should with one consent' invade the Ottoman dominions (Eden, 1555: D3r); Spanish imperial expansion will confound 'the devyll and the Turkysshe Antichryste' (Eden, 1555: A3r). Ethiopia's discovery of Christian Europe and near-simultaneous Christian engagements with Safavid Persia thus appeared to fulfil long-cherished Christian European fantasies of alliance with Christian or proto-Christian powers elsewhere in the world enshrined in the Prester John fables.[12] Reality was never so neat: instead of sending yearly tribute or uniting to crush the Ottoman foe, in 1541 the Portuguese had to militarily intervene in the country's highlands to maintain a Christian Ethiopia (Salvadore, 2010: 623).

Eden's choices and methods suggest an attempt to offer his readers as up-to-date a description of Africa as he could from the limited print sources available to him. Their primary focus on North African regions is reflected in the contours of his own account and he curiously neglects – as Blake lamented – to draw on oral sources such as the mariners and merchants providing his voyage accounts. The result is not quite the stale, haphazard mingling of classical cosmographies, antiquated mythologies, and his own fancies that has been assumed, but it does reflect Eden's willingness to privilege printed sources and their fanciful geo-humoural assumptions over contemporary intelligence, even when the two contradicted each other. In stitching together what he found to be reliable contemporary sources to supplement his own knowledge Eden created an uneven but politically astute map of the African continent that attempts to extend – unlike his sources – across its entirety, from the Mediterranean to 'the cape of *Buona Speranza*', from Guinea to Ethiopia (Eden, 1555: 345r). It again clearly demonstrates the importance of that

---

[12] Elizabeth I would send her own letter 'To the most invincible and puissant king of the Abassens, the mightie Emperour of Aethiopia the higher and the lower' with Laurence Aldersey in 1597 that was subsequently reproduced in print by Hakluyt (Hakluyt, 1598–1600: 2, 203–4).

continent to English commercial strategies. Where classical geographical terminology had been superseded, Eden attempts to note modern African usage (or at least its transliteration). Emphasis, as was typical of his sources and intellectual world view, falls upon dynastic geographies and port cities, but Eden's specific choices suggest an interest in strong African monarchies that corresponds with – but curiously does not incorporate – the admiring account of Benin in the Wyndham narrative that follows. These kingdoms were able to resist Portuguese monopolising and were thus potential English trading partners: in the terms English Guinea merchants had used to defend themselves against Portuguese accusations, places they could trade where 'the governors and the people' were 'well willing to receive us frindly and jentely' (SP 69/7 no. 449, quoted in Blake, 1942: II. 355–6).

In his 'description' Eden is also concerned with educating his audience in order that they might fully understand the implications and scope of the two voyage accounts that he subsequently reproduces. The lists of commercial centres, kingdoms, and their interconnecting rivers and deserts are augmented with rudimentary racial and religious taxonimising. The inhabitants of North Africa, or 'Asia the lesse' are 'a rusticall people' and 'are of the secte of Machomet' (Eden, 1555: 344r). Guinea and those kingdoms further to the south are 'regions of the blacke Moores cauled Ethiopians or Negros' who have 'no cities' and are 'pure Gentyles and Idolatours withowt profession of any religion or other knowledge of god then by the lawe of nature' (Eden, 1555: 344v). 'Ethiopian' can therefore be both an antiquarian 'floating signifier' and something geographically much more specific (Van Wyk Smith quoted in Young, 2015: 182). This gives rise to one of the more obvious of a series of unacknowledged contradictions in the 'breefe description': whereas general 'Ethiopians' are unequivocally identified as 'blacke Moores', the actual inhabitants of the Christian empire of Ethiopia 'are of the coloure of an olyve' (Eden, 1555: 345r), racial distinctions that reflect his confused confidence in the presiding influence of climate. Eden's human geography is further punctuated by markers that his audience could have readily placed: the 'ryver of Nilus', 'the pillars of Hercules', 'the noble citie of Carthage' (Eden, 1555: 344v). This was an act of compression designed for the use of 'al men', even if often deeply inaccurate by modern standards: as Eden notes at its end, 'to have sayde thus much of Afrike if may suffice' (Eden, 1555: 345r).

Wyndham's voyage is similarly shaped for general readers but in a different manner: here Eden imposes a moral framework through which the action is to be interpreted. Villainy is starkly heightened, an evitable result of bad character, whereas heroism lies in the resolute performance of duty in the face of monstrous injustice. Pinteado's tragic trajectory is aphoristically preset. His reputation was high at the Portuguese court, 'but as fortune in maner never favoureth but flattereth' Eden writes, perhaps reflecting on his own fortunes, 'never promyseth but decaeveth, never rayseth but casteth down ageyne, and as great wealth and favour hath alwayes companions emulation and envie', so Pinteado was forced into exile in England (Eden, 1555: 345r–345v). Similarly portentous is Eden's later reflection on a minor incident that accompanied the small fleet's eventual departure from Portsmouth:

> But first this capitayne Wyndam, puttyng furth of his shyp at Porchmouth, a kynseman of one of the headde marchauntes, and shewynge herein a muster of the tragicall partes he had conceaved in his brayne, and with such smaule begynninges nurysshed so monstrous a byrth, that more happy, yea and blessed was that younge man beinge lefte behynde then if he had byn taken with them, so sum doo wysshe he had doone the lyke by theyrs.
>
> (Eden, 1555: 345v)

Although the convolutions of his syntax make it initially difficult to follow, Eden is retrospectively identifying this otherwise fairly unremarkable moment – the setting ashore of a merchant's ill kinsman – as a point of no return for the rest of the fleet. The bounds of Wyndham's legitimate authority had already been breached and the ships, beyond royal control, were now seized by a 'tyrannie' that 'wyll rule alone' (Eden, 1555: 346r). As the focus of Wyndham's disdain and fury Pinteado became 'tormented' by this 'terrible hydra who hytherto flattered with hym and made him a faire countenance and shewe of love' (Eden, 1555: 346r): notice how Eden emphasises the upending of his position and their relationship in order to steepen the tragic trajectory. Indeed Eden carefully orchestrates a growing sense of Pinteado's victimhood, shifting tense and interjecting Wyndham's own violent diatribe against him to generate a pathos that deliberately renders the Portuguese captain almost Christlike in his goodness and resignation to suffering. Despite his ill treatment, he laments Wyndham's death 'as much as if he had byn the deerest frend he had in the worlde', but still 'certayne of the maryners and other officers dyd spette in his face, sum caulynge him Jewe' (Eden, 1555: 347v).[13] Pinteado is then forced to leave behind those English merchants stranded at the Benin court and on the return journey is 'thrust amonge the boyes of the shippe, not used like a man, nor yet like an honest boy: But glad to find favoure at the co[o]kes hande' (Eden, 1555: 348r). Thus he died, 'for very pensiveness and thowght that stroke hym to the harte' (Eden, 1555: 348r). Eden ensures that Pinteado's tragedy – and thus the tragedy of the whole voyage – insists upon

---

[13] A. F. C. Ryder speculates that this jibe may indicate that Pinteado was a *converso* (Ryder, 1969: 77 n. 1).

a reader's emotional response.[14] It becomes archetypal: here was a man 'worthy to serve any prince' who had been 'most vilely used' (Eden, 1555: 348r).

This final point is then laboriously but innovatively proven through the reproduction of a series of Portuguese court documents, perhaps the earliest English example of what Daniel Carey calls 'paratextual spaces' which provide 'a particular locus for issuing reassurances of honesty and integrity' (Carey, 2019: 528). They offer independent, regal confirmation of Pinteado's history, status, and value, but appear only after Eden takes a final opportunity to supply a further moral lesson for his readership to reflect upon. By way of introducing the documentary evidence and concluding his narrative Eden writes:

> But as the kynge of Portugale to[o] late repented hym that he had so punysshed Pinteado uppon malicious informations of such as envied the mans good fortune, even so it may hereby appere, that in sum cases, even Lyons them selves, may eyther bee hyndered by the contempt or ayded by the helpe of the pore myse accordynge unto the fable of Isope.
>
> (Eden, 1555: 348r)

Aesop's fable of the lion and the mouse was widely known across early modern Europe but readers could be forgiven for not immediately recognising the relevance of Eden's metaphor. Was the lion, initially persuaded to spare the mouse only to later be freed by it (often used as an emblem of the interconnectedness of monarch and subject), intended to signify the Portuguese king who had been as much hindered by bad counsel as well served by good? Or was the lion Pinteado, given sanctuary and employment in his exile only to be humiliated and driven to his death by these perfidious English mice? Either way the following documents are not what they appear to be. All were issued prior to Pinteado's departure to Guinea, part of the determined but ultimately unsuccessful effort undertaken by the Portuguese crown to *prevent* Pinteado joining the English fleet. Readers unaware of those specific circumstances would have had no reason to question the documents' veracity, of course, had Eden not himself undermined their authority in his rush to condemn the Portuguese. Pinteado never returned home to Portugal, he writes, because he had 'secret admonitions' that these documents were part of a wider plot 'to sley hym, if tyme and place myght have served theyr wyked intent' (Eden, 1555: 349v). As so often in this first voyage account, readers are steered by Eden's uncompromising sense of where fault and innocence lay, but are encouraged to feel that they

---

[14] The greater tragedy was that which befell the sailors of the fleet, barely mentioned in this account or by Eden. Impressed onto the ships, the minority that survived the rampant sickness and heat of the voyage returned to find George Barnes unwilling to pay them for their full service or to compensate the relatives of their dead crewmates. See Blake, 1942: II. 288 n.1.

are evaluating the narrative and its supporting evidence for themselves. In this, although he is more obviously inclined to intervention, Eden (and his printer William Powell) clearly anticipates the authorising methods and typographical format subsequently adopted by Richard Hakluyt (see Carey, 2019: 537).

3 Ivory: The Second Guinea Voyage

Eden's second English voyage account takes a completely different shape to the first. The Wyndham narrative was fashioned so that it began by educating readers in the commercial and political geographies of the African continent as accurately and succinctly as he could from the sources available to him. It then shifts register completely, as the voyage itself assumes a different generic shape, becoming a morally didactic and dramatically edifying tale that might feasibly have been retitled *The lamentable tragedy of Antonie Anes Pinteado the Portugale* and placed on the stage: although on the occasions when Eden consciously choses to deploy that term, it is Wyndham who is the 'tragicall captayne' (Eden, 1555: 346r). Indeed it was Eden's tragic histrionics that were picked up by later writers: in the extended version of his nationalistic epic poem, *Albion's England*, William Warner laconically refers to 'good *Pinteado*' who 'although an Alien' was 'abus'd / By moodie *Windam*' (Warner, 1596: 296). Throughout the account, however, Eden never loses sight of the mercantile imperatives that had generated its publication. As I have already suggested, Eden can accommodate these generic and tonal shifts within the capacious realms of 'hystory'; the second voyage, in contrast, is a detailed 'description' of 'the course of the navigation' according to 'the observation and ordinarie custime of the maryners', terms which offer a different kind of licence to author and editor (Eden, 1555: 349v).

Domestic circumstances were also very different when the second fleet departed London in early October 1554 than when Wyndham had finally left Portsmouth in August of the previous year. In February Wyatt's rebellion had been supressed and Jane Grey had been executed. In July Mary I had married Philip, King of Naples and Sicily (and, from 1556, of Spain) in Winchester. Her position now seemed secure; the succession had been resolved and English adherence to the Roman Catholic Church re-established. The strong financial return of the Wyndham voyage and continuing pressure from Portugal meant that Barne and Yorke, now in partnership with Thomas Lok and the Canary merchants Anthony Hickman and Edward Castelin, moved fast to prepare a second (Andrews, 1984: 107). Wyndham's death necessitated a change of command and the investors resolved upon John Lok, brother of Thomas and brother-in-law of Hickman, who together represented a family with deep and extensive mercantile connections. Lok's fleet of three 'goodly' ships – the *Trinity*, the *Bartholomew*, and the *John Evangelist* – and two pinnaces left London on 11 October 1554 (Eden, 1555: 349v).

Unlike the previous expedition, Lok wasted no time in fruitless skirmishing and arrived at the River Nuon/Nipoué, also known as Cestos ('Sestos' in the text), in modern-day Liberia, where his merchants busied themselves with acquiring another lucrative cargo of Malagueta pepper. They then followed Wyndham's example, trading along the Guinea coast whilst carefully avoiding the Portuguese strongholds at Elmina and Axim. Beyond those forts the local Fante population was divided into a sequence of smaller polities each with a different relationship to the Portuguese, distinctions the English were increasingly able to recognise; travelling eastward they were Ahanta, Sabeu, Commenda/Eguafo, Futu (Futo, Affuto), Sabu, Fante (Fantin/Fantyn), Aguano (Biambi), and Accra (Cracra) (Thornton, 1998: xx–xxi; Shumway, 2011a: 31). Again the English fleet sought to interpolate themselves into already established trading networks for gold and ivory. Lingering at the Ahanta town of Shama ('Samma') for four days, they sent the young Martin Frobisher ashore as a pledge of good faith and took five of the local inhabitants to be cultivated back in England as interpreters and mercantile intermediaries. Eden describes these individuals as 'certeyn blacke slaves, wherof sum were taule and strong men' (Eden, 1555: 359v) and as a consequence their acquisition is sometimes identified as part of the early stirrings of an English slave trade (for instance, Sullivan, 2020: 3–4, but see also Northrup, 2014: 6–7).

Eden's use of language here requires further comment. As far as I have been able to determine, this is the first direct association of slaves and skin colour by an English writer, or indeed of slavery with West Africa. The notion of slavery was certainly a familiar one and there are frequent earlier references to biblical and classical precedents or to slavery as a spiritual metaphor: John Bale, for instance, characteristically exhorts the faithful to 'be not a captyve slave to the lothesome kyngdom of Antichrist' (Bale, 1550: B3r). If a contemporary region is associated with slavery in these early printed books, it is invariably the Ottoman Empire and its enslavement of Christians (for instance, see Bibliander, 1542: 64r; Geuffroy, 1542: 14). Eden's *Decades* therefore represents something new, both in the density of its references to slavery (the word and its cognates appear thirty-nine times, far more than in any earlier publication) and in the locations associated with the practice. The clear majority of these references concern slavery in the Americas, with roughly equal emphasis on the Spanish enslavement of Indigenous peoples and the apparent existence of slavery in the Americas prior to European intervention.

'Black slaves' are referenced earlier in the *Decades* in Eden's close translation of a text from Ramusio, 'Of the Ilande of saynt Thomas [São Tomé] under
the Equinoctiall line', which Ramusio had in turn acquired from a Portuguese
pilot (Eden, 1555: 239v). This was no idle quotation. The Atlantic island of São
Tomé was a crucially important location for early modern conceptions of race
and slavery: one of the most prominent and lucrative of the early Portuguese
sugar plantations, it was worked by slaves from Nigeria, Kongo, and Angola
(Brooks, 2018: 122) and provided the initial basis for the transatlantic
Portuguese slave trade (Ryder, 1969: 66). Ramusio's edition refers to 'schiavi
negri' (black slaves) living there, contrasting them with the slave-owning
'mercantanti bianchi' (white merchants), a language Eden then closely reproduces in his translation of the Italian (Ramusio, 1550: 127r).[15] This earlier
appearance offers precedent but only partially explains its use in reference to the
Lok voyage. The contexts are similar: in both cases observed physiognomic
differences between those of 'hotte' African and 'coulde' European origin are
implicitly elided with polarised somatic distinctions in what appears to be an
incipient racialised discourse of black slavery. The Ahantans from Shama taken
back to England 'coulde well agree with owr meates and drynkes', Eden writes,
although the 'coulde and moyst ayer dooth sumwhat offende them' (Eden,
1555: 359v). For Eden this confirms a widely espoused geo-humoural theory
developed from its origins in the Greek Hippocratic corpus which insisted that
'latitude played a crucial role in shaping the nature of living things' (Davies,
2016: 29; see also Floyd-Wilson, 2003). In the context of European incursions
into West Africa, this theory could (and would) be used to justify abduction and
slavery: Eden explains that 'men that are borne in hotte regions may better
abyde coulde, then men that are borne in coulde regions may abyde heate,
forasmush as vehement heate resolveth the radicall moisture of mens bodies, as
could co[n]streyneth and preserveth the same' (Eden, 1555: 359v).

Yet these particular 'black slaves' were not enslaved by the English. They were
instead 'browght' to England by Lok until, as William Towerson later explained,
'they could speake the language' and then they would 'be brought againe to be
a helpe to Englishmen in this countrey' – returned, transformed, as commercial
interpreters and interlocutors (Hakluyt, 1589: 107–8).[16] Intriguingly, in doing so
the English were following Columbus's example, as reported earlier in Eden's

---

[15] The racial dynamics of São Tomé in this period are further complicated by the presence of around
     two thousand Jews deported from Portugal by João II as children in a policy which culminated
     in the expulsion of the Jews in 1496: see Brooks, 2018: 141.

[16] The same justification, perhaps influenced by the evident success of this exercise, would be given
     for the violent kidnapping of Inuit on Frobisher's voyages. See McDermott, 2001: especially
     191–3; Vaughan, 2006: 1–10; Andrea, 2016: 135–48.

Decades: ten 'Indians' had been taken by Columbus 'to lerne the Spanishe tongue, to the intent to use them afterwarde for interpretours' (Eden, 1555: 4r).[17] Again there is the suggestion of a correlation between the translation of Iberian texts and developing English mercantile practice, with Eden at its centre. At least three of the five Ahantans taken back to England – given the names George, Anthonie, and Binnie (the first two presumably christened after two of the voyage's merchant investors, George Barne and Anthony Hickman; the third named after the English transliteration of Benin) – were later returned to Shama in Towerson's subsequent voyages.[18]

At this particular historical moment at least, slavery was not the intention and, other than a market for the sale of slaves transported along the coast from Benin and elsewhere, this region was not a focus for European slaving until the second half of the seventeenth century, in quite different political circumstances (Shumway, 2011a: 33). Instead, gold, pepper, and ivory were what the English sought. The Ahantans were well aware of this – indeed the rapid expansion of the European pepper trade had already 'revolutionized existing commercial patterns' in the region (Brooks, 2018: 138) – as demonstrated in their willingness to admonish Towerson when he arrived at Shama on his first voyage of 1555–6: a local dignitary 'demaunded why we had not brought againe their men, which the last yeere we tooke away' (Hakluyt, 1589: 107).[19] Eden's use of the phrase 'black slaves' is therefore anomalous. It may be intended to imply social status: that these individuals were already in service in Shama or were intended to join the households of English merchants. Alternatively it may suggest the indiscriminate reuse of a compound familiar from his Portuguese sources that had been originally designed to specify one type of slavery at a point when many coexisted, even within the pages of Eden's volume. Its potent elision of blackness and enslavement would, in the industrialisation of the Atlantic slave trade of the following centuries, become so commonplace as to appear self-evidently true. Although this shift in emphasis and the circumstances that facilitated it were still to come, Eden's novel use of this term represents another element of his complex legacy.

When the Shaman authorities fired on the fleet, presumably acting under Portuguese influence or instruction, the English were forced to leave Frobisher

---

[17] Although less widely advertised, this had also been a Portuguese policy in West Africa from at least the 1440s (Brooks, 2018: 123).

[18] 'Bynie', 'Byne', or 'Binnie' were Anglicised versions of Benin, but geographically these terms also signified 'the whole of the coast beyond the Costa da Mina, and not the kingdom of Benin alone', hence its use in this case (Ryder, 1969: 79).

[19] A willingness to chastise European traders and hold them to their promises is evident throughout fifteenth- and sixteenth-century interactions in the region: see, for instance, Northrup, 2014: 14–16.

behind (he would be taken into Portuguese captivity before later making it back to England) and travelled with their augmented crew east. The next port of call was the Fetu town of Akong ('Cape Corea'). Formally entertained there by a local 'capitayn' named 'Don John', they exchanged the majority of their payload of cloth for gold. They then moved further east to conclude their enterprise at the Agona town of Sanya Beraku ('Perecow') on 13 February 1555. Contrary ocean currents impeded almost every stage of their homeward journey – and are discussed in detail in the account Eden reproduces – but when they did reach England twenty weeks later the voyage was celebrated as a commercial triumph. Lok had lost only twenty-four men and brought home a cargo of more than four hundred pounds of gold, thirty-six buts of pepper, and 'abowte two hundreth and fiftie elephantes teethe of all quantities' (Eden, 1555: 354r). A mark of Lok's success is that the subsequent West African voyages led by Towerson (the first of which took place the following year, 1555–6) closely followed his itinerary.

Towerson's voyages so closely mirror Lok's because he was able to draw on the accumulated experience of the previous two voyages: John Rafe (or Ralph) had sailed on the *Primrose* under Wyndham, and as navigator or master under Lok, and then became Towerson's master on the *Hector* (Alsop, 1992: 53–4). Aside from such hard-won expertise it is likely Towerson had access to some of the same records that Eden drew on for his account. There was evidently no Iberian-style embargo on sensitive mercantile intelligence in operation in England; the speed with which this material was captured in print once again implies the opposite. Such is its level of detail that the account, acquired by Eden from one of the fleet's pilots, was clearly intended to be indispensable for later adventurers. It takes the brief, episodic form of a ship's logbook but at key points it reads like a rutter (or *routier*, a card or set of instructions for finding courses at sea), with descriptions designed to instruct those that followed in the hazards, contrary currents, and distinctive details of the Guinea coast. For these sections, direct address is favoured: Cape 'Mesurado' is easily recognised 'by reason the rysinge of it is lyke a porpose hedde'; at the harbour near the mouth of the Nuon/Nipoué there are 'fyve or syxe trees that beare no leaves' and 'also a rocke in the haven mouth right as yow enter' (Eden, 1555: 351v).

As with his account of the Wyndham voyage Eden chose to keep the text's author anonymous, a decision which has the dual effect of foregrounding Eden's own control over the narrative and heightening its apparent objectivity. This may have been the obvious course of action: these records had been passed on to Eden by the voyage's commercial backers who owned and mandated them. They had been produced by the voyage, were ratified by its successful outcome, and had unimpeachable provenance, so for Eden their specific 'authorship' in a modern sense was irrelevant. In requiring and keeping such records the investors were following Spanish and Portuguese precedent where, as the Earl of Leicester's secretary would later note, they were deemed necessary in order that 'every man shall knowe his doings must come to light and judgement at Retourne' (quoted in Madox, 1976: 27). The importance of such documentary evidence was surely recognised in the immediate wake of the Wyndham debacle, had already been asserted in Eden's celebration of Spanish methods, and would only increase thereafter. Nevertheless, the keeping of logbooks was still something of a novelty by Lok's voyage, and his is one of the earliest examples, alongside that of Hugh Willoughby in 1553.[20] Sebastian Cabot had first advocated their use for English voyages in 1549, and they are particularly prominent in northern expeditions, again suggesting the importance of Cabot and emerging Muscovy Company practice for these early West African voyages (see Schotte, 2013: 287). Eden would therefore have been familiar with the form and the purpose it served: his innovation was to use the logbook template as the basis for his published account, taking what was a commercial/navigational document and reforming it for a wider readership.

Once the logbook had been established as its core foundation, Eden proceeded to embroider and augment the account. Miscellaneous observations from 'our crew' are added, as are Eden's own, alongside extensive quotation from classical and contemporary sources. An uneasy polyvocality is again created, more disorienting than that in the Wyndham narrative, and the identity of specific voices is blurred in order that all can share in the didactic authority of the predominating logbook account. This has led to a prevailing critical uncertainty over who is speaking and when, a confusion only heightened when the account was later reproduced by Hakluyt, whose running heads attribute the first voyage to 'Windam' and the second to 'Robert Gainsh', with only the 'breefe description' ascribed to Eden (Hakluyt, 1589: 83–98). The result has often been the effacing of Eden, a logical result of his strategic creation of what Mary Fuller calls the account's 'complex authorship' (Fuller, 2019: 345 n. 8). The Lok account's intermixture of the deeply technical with practical instruction, metaphorical reflection, and further excursions into geography, ethnography, and natural history would go on to influence many of the English voyage narratives published in the years that followed.[21]

---

[20] Wiloughby's logbook was recovered when the remains of his party were discovered on the Kola Penninsular in 1554. It is reproduced in Hakluyt, 1589: 267–70.

[21] That influence appears in those accounts collected by Hakluyt that were crafted for publication (rather than the purely commercial/navigational material that is also abundant) but is perhaps most apparent in accounts of the English engagements in the north-west, such as George Best's account of the ill-fated Frobisher voyages, *A True Discourse of the Late Voyages of Discoverie* (1578).

Despite its melodramatics, Eden's account of Wyndham's voyage had been narrated in a relatively straightforward linear style, supplemented by his preceding introduction to contemporary European knowledge of Africa. Eden's presentation of Lok's voyage is strikingly different, and this cannot be explained solely by the nature and centrality of the logbook. Once the navigational information had been included and the fleet's basic movements recorded, Eden broke with convention to abruptly terminate the narrative, abandoning Lok and his fleet on the West African coast. He turned instead 'to speake sumwhat of the contrey and people, and of suche thynges as are browght from thense' (Eden, 1555: 354r). What follows is a sequence of apparent digressions that profoundly shift the tone of the account. Ostensibly added to flesh out the spartan, coordinate-driven logbook narrative, they vary considerably in terms of their specificity, their reliance on and fidelity to prior sources, and in the extent of Eden's input and that of Lok's crews. Digressions of this type were not unusual, even in much earlier writing on travel and geography. Herodotus is an obvious model, and like Herodotus there is clear craft at work in Eden's assembly of this account: following the logbook material, a reader is given a very specific account of the fauna of the region and its uses, followed by another ethno-geographical account of Africa, this time taken directly (as Eden acknowledges) from Gemma Frisius (Frisius, 1530: 84–5), then a speculative consideration of the African climate, before a concluding tableau of observations taken from the returned English mariners. Each informs the next and the earlier sections set up the final part as a meaningful contribution to English and wider European knowledge on West Africa.

Yet beyond their narratological function some of these short pieces develop a discursive, reflective, and personalised style that in such respects anticipate Montaigne's *Essais* (first published in 1580).[22] This element of Eden's book has consequently bewildered historians and literary critics, who have recognised its '*almost* lyrical' qualities (my emphasis: Hall, 1995: 50) but who find it 'fantastical' where it should be factual (Olusoga, 2016: 53) and epistemologically unstable: it is 'of uncertain origin and value' (Fage, 1980: 50). The best example of this kind of writing comes immediately after the sudden closure of the logbook account. Having left Lok and his fleet off the Ahantan coast, Eden jumps forward in time to the aftermath of their return and the inventorying of their cargo. For the first time he explicitly becomes his readers' intermediary, weighing and appraising on their behalf. Of the 'elephantes teeth of all quantities' Eden writes that he 'sawe and measured sum of .ix. spannes in length and

---

[22] See, for instance, the similar conclusions drawn by Montaigne and Eden at the conclusion of the former's essay 'On a monster-child' (Montaigne, 2003: 808).

they were crokede. Sum of them were as bygge as a mans thygh about the knee: and weyed abowte foure score and ten pounde weyght a piece'. He saw others 'which they caule the teeth of calves of one or two or three yeares, wherof sum were a foote and a halfe, summe two foote, and sum three or more accordynge to thage of the beast' (Eden, 1555: 354r). The specifics are important, for they enable Eden to anchor what might otherwise be a flight of wonder in concrete facts. Myths of monstrosity are being self-consciously replaced by observable, measurable, provable data. It is on this basis that he can correct 'the paynters and arras woorkers' of an earlier age who had depicted elephants with tusks growing 'in the nether jawe upwarde' rather than 'the upper jawe downewarde' (Eden, 1555: 354r).

Scale, and an appreciation of the mechanics involved in producing it, leads to further reflection. In addition to the ivory the Lok voyage had returned with 'the headde of an elephante of such huge byggenesse' that Eden estimates in its living state it 'coulde wey lyttle lesse then fyve hundreth weyght'. This head was put on display in the London house of the merchant (and earlier Mayor of London) Sir Andrew Judde where 'dyvers' had crowded in to see it. The spectacle prompts Eden to issue a revealing observation that is simultaneously a critique of his fellow gawpers. He had also been to Judde's house to see the skull, but he:

> behelde it not onely with my bodely eyes, but much more with the eyes of my mynde and spirite consydered by the woorke, the cunnynge and wysedome of the woorke master: withowt which consyderation, the syght of such straunge and woonderfull thynges may rather seeme curiosities then profitable con-templations. (Eden, 1555: 354r)

Here Eden presents a further justification for what he imagines as an intellec-tually and spiritually engaged English expansionism. If the surplus theory espoused early in his book had shown on a global scale how the earth had been divinely created in such a way that only commerce could bring it together, Eden's sense that acquiring close and detailed knowledge of that world (again through trade) could reveal the hand of a divine architect complemented that project on a more tactile, tangible level. In arguing that the gap between 'curiosity' and 'profitable contemplation' (with a useful slippage between spiritual and financial profit) lay solely in different ways of seeing, Eden also provided a rationale for his editing and inclusion of these first English voyage narratives, and for the volume as a whole. He produces and shapes the various accounts in order to communicate an expanding world, but he expects active readers to fully comprehend their meaning and the divine plan underpinning them. In short, Eden seeks to make the strange profitable in commercial, political, spiritual, and literary terms.

The same rationale explains the substantial and detailed discussion of elephants to which these personalised reflections lead. Its inclusion is less concerned with participating in 'the mystification of Africa' (indeed Eden argues that he doing the opposite), or even consciously engaging in a capitalist *re*mystification of the continent (Olusoga, 2016: 53). Rather the sole reason for this passage is ivory. Lok had returned with what Alice Kleist suggests was 'the greatest haul recorded by any single expedition' up to that date (Kleist, 1957: 66).[23] The London market was now glutted with a raw material it did not yet have the capacity to fully process.[24] Much would presumably have been sold on to European markets, likely through Antwerp or Nuremberg, but at least a portion remained in England. There are clear signs in the remaining records of the impact of this influx of ivory. Although only one of the Marian rolls survives detailing the traditional ritual of New Year gift giving at court, from 1557, it contains far more references to ivory than any subsequent roll in the rest of the century, where the records are complete. In Latin ivory is *ebuneae*; in the English inventories it often features as ebonett or ibonett (Lawson, 2013: 579). In 1557 Mary I was given a series of comb cases made of or inlayed with ebonett and containing combs of ebonett (high-status combs were almost always made of ivory in this period: see the contemporary royal example in Figure 3) by her noblewomen, as well as 'a Cheir of Ebonett covered with Cremsen vellat and fringed with silke and golde' by 'Jacob Ragoson', or Giacomo Ragazzoni, a distinguished Italian merchant based in Venice (BL Add. MS 62525).[25] As one of the most prominent of the early Barbary and Guinea investors, the Yorke family were particularly adept at using these occasions to celebrate and advocate for their trade. To Mary, Lady Yorke had presented six 'suger lo[a]ves' as well as figs and suckets; with sugar a key import from the Barbary states (suckets, or succades, were fruits preserved in sugar: BL Add. MS 62525). In 1559, the first New Year festivities of the reign of the new Queen Elizabeth I, she would seek to retain courtly favour for herself and her husband with something similar. It was 'a Combe case of Ibonett' that was, as with earlier examples, presumably 'furnisshed' with decorated combs of ivory,

---

[23] Although Lok's cargo of around two hundred and fifty tusks was dwarfed by the five hundred 'ollyffants teithe' carried from 'Gyney' by a French ship blown by a storm onto the Sussex coast in early 1560. Francis Edwards to William Cecil, 2 February 1560: SP 70/11/3r. English interest in Guinea had been registered from around 1480 (Blake, 1942: II. 263) and William Hawkins had brought a smaller amount of ivory back to Plymouth in 1540: see Andrews, 1984: 59.

[24] The major revival of European ivory carving would not take place until the beginning of the following century: see Hecht, 2008 and Bassanio and Fagg, 1988.

[25] Mary was given comb cases and combs by Lady Isabel Radcliffe, Lady Elizabeth Catesby, and Mistress Mary Dannet: BL Add. MS 62525, 1557. Ragazzoni had left Venice for London around 1542 and would ride in Mary I's coronation procession. He returned to Italy in 1558 and travelled to the Ottoman court in 1571. My thanks to Tom Roberts for this information.

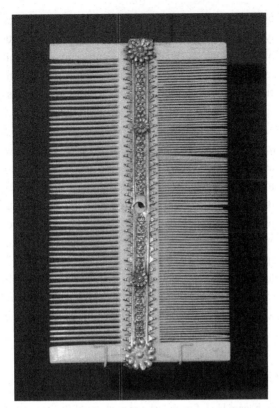

Figure 3 Double-sided ivory comb from the Royal Collection, *c.*sixteenth century. RCIN 37050. Royal Collection Trust / © Her Majesty Queen Elizabeth II 2022

accompanied with 'a vane [fan] wrought with silke and glass of the same' (Lawson, 2013: 59.86).[26] Just as artisanal craft transformed elephants' teeth into items suitable for royalty, creating an elaborate material plea for the continuance of the West African trade, so Eden fashions a discourse on the nature and origins of that unfamiliar raw material in order to translate it – to render it familiar and to stabilise its value – for an English readership.

To do so he turned first to Pliny the Elder's *Naturalis historia*. Framing new knowledge required, as Eden's earlier 'breefe description of Affrike' had demonstrated, a reliance on established authorities; ideally a balance of the contemporary and the classical, in accordance with earlier humanistic approaches. Pliny was indisputably an authority in this area – with more direct experience of live elephants than Eden – and his book 'was one of the single best-sellers of the

---

[26] For later examples of gifts of ivory combs in cases see Lawson, 2013: 84.136.

early printed book trade' (Cummings, 2004: 171). Yet Eden does not simply reproduce Pliny word for word, as he subsequently does with Frisius on African geographies. Instead he judiciously selects relevant sections, scrambling the order of the original as he mixes in anecdotal and eyewitness information.

The result, certainly for twenty-first-century readers, is a curious amalgam of proto-zoological facts – size, kind, behaviour – and the mythic – for instance, Eden quotes Pliny in full on the perpetual battle between elephants and dragons. This episode was presumably retained because it was so well known that it had long become anecdotal (see Figure 4), with the added benefit that this apparently implausible feud generated something concrete: as Eden explains, it is from the 'mengeled' blood of the two dying beasts that the 'substaunce which the apothecaries caule *Sanguis Draconis*, (that is) dragons blud, otherwyse cauled *Cinnabaris*' comes (Eden, 1555: 355r: although there was some contemporary scepticism regarding this connection – see Madox, 1976: 228). Where possible, assertions are again buttressed with eyewitness observation. After quoting Philostratus on the characteristics of 'the Ethiope or Guinea' elephant (presumably the African forest elephant, *Loxodonta cyclotis*) Eden assures his readers that 'owr men sawe one drynkyng at a ryver in Guinea as they sayled into the lande' (Eden, 1555: 355r).

Having been thoroughly educated in the best information available on the morphology of the live elephant, readers are returned to the uses of the raw material with which Eden began. He references the many uses of 'Ivery or elephantes teeth' in classical 'oulde tyme'. From it was made 'tables, tressels, postes of houses, rayles, lattesses for wyndowes, Images of theyr goddes, and dyvers other thynges' (Eden, 1555: 355r). This celebration of versatility is simultaneously an inventory of possibilities now that England has entered the trade so successfully. After all, he notes, there was continuity: the ancients made 'goodly workes' of ivory 'intermyxte with sundry kyndes of precious wooddes, as at this day are made certeyne chayres, lutes, and virginalles' (Eden, 1555: 355r). Eden finds that ivory was so plentiful in the ancient world that its metaphors suffused classical culture, its fabled whiteness informing conceptions of race. It was so abundant,

> that (as farre as I remember) Josephus wryteth that one of the gates of Hierusalem was cauled *Porta Eburnea*, (that is) the Ivery gate. The whytenesse thereof was so muche esteemed that it was thought to represent the naturall fayrenesse of mans skynne: In so much that such as went abowt to set furth (or rather corrupte) naturall bewtie with colours and payntynge, were reproved by this proverbe: *Eber atramento candefacere*. That is: To make Ivery whyte with ynke. The poettes also describynge the fayre neckes of bewtifull virigins, caule them *Ebernea colla*: That is: Ivery neckes. (Eden, 1555: 355v)

Figure 4 An elephant fighting a dragon, from a thirteenth-century theological miscellany. BL Harley MS 3244, f. 39v. By permission of the British Library

Kim Hall has written perceptively about this passage and suggests that it 'works to establish whiteness as a cultural value through a series of displacements' (Hall, 1995: 51). She argues that for Eden the 'posited ideal – the white, male, "classical" body – is the constant referent . . . and always projected as beautiful' (Hall, 1995: 52). Yet to Hall the prevailing feeling is nevertheless 'unease about the reliability of whiteness as a stable register of value' (Hall, 1995: 51), unease triggered by Eden's reference to 'painting' the white female body.

Whilst I broadly agree with Hall, I want to suggest that the unease runs considerably deeper and emerges from a different source. Eden's reflections here continue a preoccupation with race that is apparent throughout the *Decades*, something he half acknowledges later in the same account. Although he generally subscribes to geo-humoural theory in order to explain the production of racial diversity in the world, upon completing Eden's book a reader is left with more questions than answers. As he later accepts, geo-humouralism cannot yet fully explain why, for instance, 'throughout all Afryke under the Equinoctiall line and neare abowt the same on bothe sydes, the regions are extreeme hotte and the people very blacke' whereas those of the same latitude in the West Indies are 'of the coloure of an olyve'. This apparent contradiction is ultimately left as a 'secreate woorke of nature' (Eden, 1555: 359v). In this he follows another of the sources he excerpts in the *Decades*, Francisco López de Gómara's *Historia de las Indias y conquista de Mexico*. Gómara had asserted that 'one of the marveylous thynges that god useth in the composition of man, is coloure'. For him human variety was as inexplicable as it was astonishing: the appearance of 'dyvers sortes of whytenesse', 'dyvers maners of yelowe', 'dyvers sortes of blacknesse' and all shades in between seemed to defy any scholarly rationale (Eden, 1555: 310v). Those 'phyloso-phers' in search of an ultimate cause had little choice but to 'consyder that his divine majestie hath doonne this' in a declaration of his 'omnipotencie and wisdome' (Eden, 1555: 311r). Eden was therefore well aware of the deficiencies of the established rationales for race and, in foregrounding these problems, he engages the reader in his attempt to assay different models and language that might better explain the matter.[27] The fabled whiteness of ivory provides an opportunity to reflect upon classical ideals but, unlike elsewhere in the volume where classical knowledge is both authoritative and valuable in the present, in this passage Eden is careful to distance earlier notions of 'naturall' whiteness

---

[27] Later in the century the same question led Abraham Hartwell to fervently wish that 'some sound *Naturall Philosopher*, such as *Fernelius* that wrote *De abditis rerum causis*, or as *Levinus Lemnius de Occultis Naturae miraculis*, or as *Franciscus Valesius de Sacra Philosophia*, would enter into the *Closet* of *Contemplation*, to finde out the true *Naturall* cause' of 'these colours in humane bodies' (Lopes, 1597: *3v).

through his consistent recourse to the past tense: they 'had'; 'it was thought'. In effect this establishes a distinction between antiquarian conceptions of an assumed 'naturall' human whiteness and a widespread sixteenth-century acceptance that all somatic difference was produced by 'naturall' geo-humoural processes.

Similarly revealing is the instability of Eden's authorial/editorial authority in these lines. From the opening sentence he is uncharacteristically tentative and unusually foregrounds his own unreliability in parenthesis: '(as far as I remember)'. This gives a further hint of the speed with which this account must have been assembled, but it also represents a shift in tone that is only heightened by the fact that Eden *is* misremembering. The ivory gate, mentioned by Homer rather than Josephus, is in Hades not Jerusalem (and is often associated with the *Porta Eburnea* in Perugia. See Homer's *Odyssey*, 1919 ed: Bk. 19, ll. 563–4).[28] The proverb with which those who sought to corrupt their 'naturall bewtie' were admonished, *ebur atramento candefacere*, is also more ambivalent than Eden suggests, for it originates in an argument at the dressing table of Philematium, a recently freed courtesan, in Plautus's satirical play *Mostellaria*. Hers is not the uncorrupted natural beauty Eden implies. Furthermore although it may be intended, as Hall suggests, as an 'evocation' of the Biblical *Song of Songs*, the more literal and most celebrated example of a poet's use of *eburnea colla*, as Eden would have been well aware, comes from the fateful moment of Narcissus's self-adoration in Ovid's *Metamorphoses* (Ovid, 1916 ed: Bk. 3, l. 422). Following his rejection of Echo, Nemesis had entrapped Narcissus with his own beauty. So rather than any 'bewtifull virgin' these words refer to the 'false' reflection with which Narcissus became mortally intoxicated.

Cumulatively these three mistaken, ill-fitting, or ambivalent allusions confirm Hall's point about Eden's 'unease' with using whiteness 'as a stable register of value', but they imply a more fundamental fracture. If Eden's aim in this passage was to establish a coherent, fixed conception of whiteness back in a static, exemplary classical past, from which it could inform notions of race in the present, then he failed. It seems that whiteness was always an unstable referent. Indeed Eden only seems confident in discussing race on those occasions when he can point to a monochromatic, 'elemental difference between black and white bodies' without the need for elaborate taxonomies or further explanation (Hall, 1995: 52 n. 21). As elsewhere in an early modern English society struggling to comprehend a world that was changing and expanding, conceptions of racial difference were either absolute – Gómara's 'coloures utterlye contrarye' – or they threatened to collapse entirely (Eden, 1555: 310v).

---

[28] Ivory does feature prominently in Josephus, in particular as the material of Solomon's throne, but not as a building material for Jerusalem. See the corresponding passage in 1 Kings 10:18.

Contradictions remain in the final sections concerned with the Lok voyage. Eden's focus moves away from ivory and elephants to a consideration of what he calls 'the woonders and monstrous thynges that are engendered in Afrike' (Eden, 1555: 359r). The narrative oscillates uncertainly between the general and the highly specific in its attempt to inform and delight the reader, but it resolutely retains its Guinean and commercial rationales. First Eden inserts a lengthy section on the peoples of Africa in order to provide further information on those 'whiche nowe inhabite the regions of the coast of Guinea' as well as other areas, which he notes 'were in oulde tyme cauled Ethiopes and Nigrite, which we nowe caule Moores, Moorens, or Negroes, a people of beastly lyvynge, without a god, lawe, religion, or common welth' (Eden, 1555: 355v). Here is another direct contradiction of the evidence of the two preceding English accounts, which had clearly affirmed the existence of political structures at local and state levels, as well as established commercial networks with which they could engage: indeed the English justification for their own presence in the region in response to Portuguese objections depended upon both. Again we see the kinds of double-speak common to this and later English voyage accounts in which long-established cosmographical paradigms are blithely spliced together with new geographies and eyewitness accounts even when they were entirely incompatible. The resulting cognitive dissonance, in part a consequence of the lack of any established generic template for this kind of writing, also suggests that Eden was credulous regarding Africa in ways he was not in other contexts (for instance, the far north) although such provocative incongruities almost invariably accompany the presentation of new knowledge in sixteenth-century travel writing. Eden puts the same point slightly differently. The strange wonders of nature he presents to his readers lead him to 'consyder and caule to rememberaunce the narrownes of mans understandynge and knowleage in comparyson of her mighty poure [power]'. Reaching for classical authority even as he acknowledges its limitations, he 'can but cease to marvayle and confesse with Plinie that nothynge is to her impossible, the leaste parte of whose poure is not yet knowen to men' (Eden, 1555: 357v–358r).

Accordingly Frisius's brief rehearsal of the monstrous races of Africa, including further invocation of Prester John and punctuated by Eden's own updating interjections, is followed by a return to the material gathered on Lok's voyage. Africa is depicted as a repository of extreme meteorological phenomena, each of which Eden treats as an intellectual problem to be resolved. Thus reports of 'fyery exhalations' in the African night accompanied by the 'sounde of pipes, trumpettes, and droomines' can be explained through recourse to 'common and dayly experience' which 'teacheth us' that fire makes noise as it moves through the air, as with a gun or a burning torch

(Eden, 1555: 357r). Some 'of owre men of good credit that were in this last vyage to Guinea' similarly affirmed that 'they felt a sensible heate to comme from the beames of the moone'. Again Eden finds an explanation, this time in his knowledge of the composition of heavenly bodies, but here, intriguingly, a note of cultural relativism, conditioned by geography, begins to appear: this might seem 'straunge and insensible to us that inhabite coulde regions' he writes, but such observations accord with the fact that the nature of all 'starres and planets (as wryteth Plinie) consysteth of fyre, and conteyneth in it a spiritie of lyfe, whiche cannot be without heate' (Eden, 1555: 357 r–357v). As is the case throughout his additions to these two English voyages, Eden's intention is to encourage a reader's sense of wonder, a word that he frequently uses but which he deliberately unmoors from its earlier association with a thrill of incomprehension in the face of the unknown. Eden was in the vanguard of what Jonathan Sell has identified as an early modern 'transition from a metaphorical to an empirical episteme' (Sell, 2006: 49). For him wonder was a useful emotional response that could be manipulated as 'a stimulus to cognition' (Sell, 2006: 4), eliciting an intense engagement from his readers whilst cultivating and expanding their consciousness of the world.

Things become more specific as Eden moves to consider West African 'maners' such as the practice of 'princes and noble men' to 'pounse and rase theyr skynnes with prety knottes in divers formes as it were branched damaske, *thynkynge* that to be a decent ornament' (my emphasis: Eden, 1555: 358r).[29] This recognition of different aesthetic tastes more pointedly introduces a Herodotan note of cultural relativism that in both cases uses 'manners' or custom as a means to recognise, and perhaps even undermine, ethnocentricity. Herodotus famously used the Persian king Darius's revelation of the mutual disgust of the Greeks and the Callatian Indians at each other's death rituals to reflect that 'use and wont is lord of all'. Eden grudgingly comes to a similar conclusion, perhaps unwittingly confirming Herodotus's accompanying dictum that 'if it were proposed to all nations to choose which seemed best of all customs, each, after examination made, would place its own first' (Herodotus, 1921: Bk. 3, 51). He carries this notion, all the time testing it for any commercial advantage it might bring, into a consideration of female body adornment. In doing so, Eden once again takes on the role of physical intermediary:

> I my selfe have one of theyr braselettes of Ivery wayinge . . . .xxxviii. ounces. This, one of theyr women dyd weare upon her arme. It is made of one hole

---

29 The same practice is later noted by Richard Hawkins (Hakluyt, 1589: 526) and Richard Madox (Madox, 1982: 191–2), amongst others.

piece of the byggest parte of the toothe turned and sumwhat carved, with a hole in the myddest wherin they put theyr handes to weare it on theyr arme. Sum have of every arme one and as many on theyr legges, wherewith sum of theym are so galded that althoughe they are in maner made lame therby, yet wyll they by no meanes leave them of. Sum weare on theyr legges great shackels of bryght copper which *they thynke* to bee no less cumly. (my emphasis: Eden, 1555: 358r)

The tactile immediacy with which Eden describes his handling of the ivory armlet indicates the value he accords it. However, his evident lack of interest in the inscribed decoration – 'sumwhat carved' – suggests that he is more concerned with the quantity of raw material than in the armlet as a cultural artefact (for examples of these extraordinary items and their elaborate ornamentation, see Bassani and Fagg, 1988). Even so, one of the uses of ivory for Eden beyond its material worth to elite European consumers was its useful position at a confluence of economic and cultural value systems, its apparently universal appeal making it an ideal vehicle to bring West Africa into England and the English imagination. His critique of those women who seem to suffer for their vanity misunderstands the import of copper *manillas*, worn by women to display the wealth of their households, but it is also interestingly cross-cultural: the sixteenth century expansion and intensification of global trade generated sartorial anxieties that were routinely displaced onto women and the young, from Japan and the Ottoman Empire to London (see Rublack, 2010: 7–15; Dimmock, 2019: 224).

Eden's use of the word 'shackels' is notable in this context: the word's prior usage in English (and in Eden's book) always refers to fetters for prisoners, but after Eden it begins to incorporate jewellery and accessories like the armlets and anklets indicated in this passage (*Oxford English Dictionary n.* 1.3). The final objects in his litany of female adornment give a clearer sense of the nature of Eden's acquisitive gaze. Some women, he adds, 'weare on theyr bare armes certeyne foresleeves made of the plates of beaten golde' and on their fingers 'they weare rynges made of golden wyres'. The very last items he lists are particularly intriguing. In exchange for their English wares, he writes, 'owr men bowght of them ... certeyne dogges chaynes and collers' of pure gold (Eden, 1555: 358r). Are we to take his description literally, in which case a reader is given a powerful impression of the wealth of West Africa, as well, perhaps, as the extent to which the English had debased themselves in their desire for precious metals? Al-Wazzan's *Geographical historie* described the king of 'Borno' (Kanem-Bornu) as 'marveilous rich', for 'his spurres, his bridles, platters, dishes, pots, and other vessels wherein his meate and drinke are brought to the table, are all of pure golde: yea, and the chaines of his dogs and hounds are of gold also' (al-Wazzan, 1600: 294), but there is no evidence for such canine ostentation in those West African regions Lok visited in this period. It may be that Eden is translating jewellery into a form his readers would readily understand, although he or his typesetter did choose to highlight the term 'dog chaines of golde' in the text's margin, as did the subsequent editions of Willes and Hakluyt (Eden, 1555: 358r; Willes, 1577: 351r; Hakluyt, 1589: 96), implying at least some took the prospect seriously.

Whether he was swayed by a vision of English merchants lusting after dog collars or not, Eden's text then pivots in a different direction. Earlier he had encouraged a perception of the inhabitants of Guinea as a rootless, wandering people without culture, government, or religion. Now he advises his readers and those traders who intended to follow Wyndham and Lok that these 'are very ware [wary] people in theyr bargenynge, and wyl not lose one sparke of golde of any value'; they are also scrupulously precise in their use of weights and measures. Indeed, those intending to trade must leave their English vices behind: the people of Guinea must be treated 'gentelly' for 'they wyl not trafike or brynge in any wares if they be evyll use[d]' (Eden, 1555: 358r). The example Eden gives is revealing. On Wyndham's voyage one of the crew had 'eyther stole a muske catte or tooke her a way by force' during their first stop at the mouth of the River Nuon/Nipoué ('Sestos'), blithely assuming that there would be no consequences. Yet no matter how rapidly they sailed on along the coast, 'the fame of theyr mysusage so prevented the[m] that the people of that place also offended therby, wold bring in no wares: In so muche that they were inforced eyther to restore the catte or pay for her at theyr price before they could trafike there' (Eden, 1555: 358v).

Implicit in Eden's relation of these English difficulties is a sense of reckoning. Everything about Wyndham's voyage indicates that the fleet carried with them a set of assumptions about West African indigeneity that corresponded with some of the material Eden had reproduced in his descriptive passages: that the people they expected to deal with were mired in a 'barbarousness' that made them atomised and disparate, lacking even basic social structures or any commercial sophistication. Instead they found themselves confronted by their own erroneous stereotypes and by a connected culture that expected fair and equitable trading practices and people who were quite prepared to demand the promised return of their compatriots. The episode of the civet cat was both a warning and an admonition: this was not the easy capitulation the rapacious English had expected. It also places the text in a curiously liminal position in terms of European conceptions of Africa. Here Eden offers an unequivocal assertion of the economic sophistication of West African merchants that the Portuguese had long recognised, a sophistication that largely displaces lingering assertions of African barbarism in the text. It did not last very long. Rather than herald a new model of mercantile interaction, this recognition was itself within a century displaced by 'an urgent need to refute the idea that inhabitants of the West African coast possessed economic rationality' in the process of 'assigning rational primacy to European mercantilism' (Morgan, 2021: 136). In this sense the *Decades* is a relic of a point when alternative models of engagement were still in circulation.

The Lok account concludes with a flurry of detail, focussing on the prodigious flora and fauna 'engendered' in Africa alongside other proto-ethnographic materials. Eden reports on the composition of houses, the viability of 'flyinge fysshes' for sustenance at sea, the distinctive Guinean practice of baking bread, the marvellous size of African wheat (which Eden had personally examined), and the usefulness of the 'Palmites' tree. All are linked through 'the fervent heate' of the sun, which causes those peoples subjected to it 'such greefes and molestations' but which generates an extraordinary 'frutefulnesse' in everything else. For Eden these contrary solar effects are another cause for reflection: it is 'doubtlesse a woorthy contemplation' on 'the contrary passions of suche thynges as receave thinfluence of his beames eyther to theyr hurte or benefite' (Eden, 1555: 359r).

The excessive generative power of Africa seems in Eden's account to leave nothing untouched. He draws to a close with a description of the ships from both the Wyndham and Lok voyages incapacitated because they have been 'marvelously overgrowe[n] with certein shels of .ii. ynches length and more as thycke' (perhaps the large *Megabalanus tintinnabulum* native to West Africa) and 'in many places eaten with the woormes cauled Bromas or Bissas' (Teredo worms, from the family *Teredinidae*). Eden describes seeing Wyndham's *Primrose* 'lying in the docke', presumably laid on its side in the process of being careened, encrusted in teeming, unclassifiable, West African life, after it had limped back to England with only a fraction of its original crew. There could not have been a more stark confirmation of his theory that the African sun purged and scorched some lives even as it supercharged others. The only parallel he provides is telling: such shells 'have [also] byn seene' on English ships 'returning from Islande' (Eden, 1555: 359v). Iceland was another region associated with untrammelled natural forces in the European imagination – and the destination of an established long-distance English shipping route with which Eden was likely to have been familiar – but even its invasive northern fauna had been surpassed by the size and extent of this African encrustation and its accompanying worms (see Jones, 2000: 105–10).

In Eden's hands the Lok voyage had become something strikingly experimental, much more so than his generically straightforward shaping of the

Wyndham account. Its disjunctions and digressions complicate a reader's sense of narrative; its movement from detailed, linear navigation into looping, reflective passages culminates with a Guinean tableau in which sequences of loosely connected items, impressions, and behaviours are related in order to spur readerly contemplation. Above all Eden expected his readers to consider the mysterious nature of God's work and its slow revelation, which for him required a recognition of one's own situatedness in the world that could only come through exposure to its variety and diversity. This was a nationalistically inflected departure from the Martyr and Ramusio models, and from earlier travel writing that is rarely so attentive to the reading experience. In the final section of his Lok account, Eden explicitly addressed this defining concern, which frames his relation of both English Guinea voyages. Once again he presented his work as a necessary act of memorialisation: he 'thought good' to put some of the crews' observations 'in memory' in order that 'the reader may aswell take pleasure in the varietie of thynges as knowleage of the hystory' (Eden, 1555: 358r).[30] Close attention to these factors, the connective tissue of the account, has laid bare how it was Eden's idiosyncratic mingling of his own sense of duty with a desire to provoke, pleasure, and teach his readers against a highly charged English political backdrop that produced such compellingly complex and fractured voyage material. It, in turn, fulfilled his aim of generating new ways of reading and thinking about the world.

Conclusions

This much we know: towards the end of his 1555 translation and augmentation of Peter Martyr's *Decades* Richard Eden incorporated the first two Tudor voyage accounts to appear in print. They were by his own admission added late in the process, and the return of the Lok voyage in the year of publication, plus some signs of haste in the text, suggest both were assembled fairly rapidly. Their inclusion had been enjoined by certain 'freindes' keen – I suggest – to make the case for continuing English trade to Guinea in the face of firm Portuguese opposition and the aggressive state intervention that followed. One obvious consequence of these circumstances is a strong antipathy to Portuguese imperial pretentions, in West Africa and more broadly. The rejection of the Portuguese accusations embedded in the substance of the two accounts enables Eden to further develop and articulate an English expansionist ideology that was now more commercial than colonial in its emphasis: that worked around, between, and within Iberian spheres of influence that with the Marian

---

[30] For more on remembering and its centrality to representations of the early modern voyage, see Fuller, 2008: 1–20.

accession were now an immoveable and immediate reality for English merchants and mariners.

It is also clear that Eden's book – and I would argue, contrary to cataloguing convention, that it is Eden's rather than Martyr's book – was intended to be read by multiple constituencies. It is addressed directly to Mary and Philip as a celebration of Spanish imperial greatness and of the potential influence of that greatness in England. As Hadfield has demonstrated, this pro-colonial stance sits uneasily with the tone of the volume as a whole: Eden praises the conquistadores 'in a manner that is alien to both Peter Martyr's preface and his actual text' (Hadfield, 1995/6: 14). In celebrating Spain he sought to gain influence on the direction of English foreign policy. The book was also designed to encourage courtly patrons and speak to the needs and concerns of English merchants and sailors, exhorting them to action, offering valuable geographical, navigational, and commercial intelligence. Finally, it attempted to appeal to a more heterogeneous and unpredictable body of educated general readers, and publication marks a primary difference between Eden's voyage material and the simpler, more direct, contemporaneous account of the Chancellor voyage written by Clement Adams. In return for their purchase Eden's readers were promised variety, entertainment, and edification.

Narrative form is at the heart of Eden's innovation. Once he had resolved to build his book upon the translation of Martyr's text he was bound into a substantial body of writing that attempted to communicate and give shape to accounts of the 'New Worlds' of the Americas. There was, as I have already noted, no established form for printed voyage narratives in English before the late sixteenth century: readers needed to be engaged and educated. This was new literary ground, 'a strangely eclectic blend of chronological narrative, description of landscapes, justifications of military actions, political interpretations, and anthropological curiosity over the customs, beliefs, and social practices of the native population' (Brennan, 1996/7: 228). In a practical sense this meant that Eden was not bound by any formal restrictions or expectations beyond the centrality of the eyewitness account: that these voyage accounts were the first of their kind in English, and the inaugural documents of a newly established Guinea trade, gave him even greater freedom. Alongside the logbook template, newly established in England by Sebastian Cabot and used for the Lok voyage, Eden constructed his published account from a wide range of raw materials: unofficial, verbal retellings, commercial documents, his interviews of senior crew members, and his own observations and interactions with ships, sailors, and commercial goods. To all these materials Eden brought his secretarial experience in assessing, paring, and establishing a narrative as well as his extensive knowledge of relevant classical literature – Ptolomy,

Herodotus, Pliny – and his reading of contemporary travel and geographical writing – Martyr, Münster, Ramusio, and especially Frisius.

Eden's eccentric navigation of the complex political situation and the unevenness of his sources, the malleability of the form, and his management of the expectations of his different readers led to two highly distinct narratives of English exploration. The first develops a fatalistic tone by fashioning the fleet's admiral as an absolute villain and his Portuguese deputy as a monstrously ill-used innocent. Aside from a few vivid descriptive details, the Guinea coast and their commercial mission seem little more than a backdrop to the playing out of this tragic Christian European dynamic, with the disintegration of the Kurtz-like Wyndham accelerated with every mile he moves away from English subjecthood. In total contrast, in Eden's second sea voyage account a reader is told nothing of the commander or of shipboard dynamics. The spare efficiency and rigorous linearity of the logbook source gave Eden licence to abruptly discard consecutive narrative when it suited him, shifting focus and orientation to encourage close reflection on material goods, West African customs, climatological differences, and the contingencies and historical instabilities of Christian European conceptions of race.

When read as two halves of a 'hystory' of the new Guinea trade, as Eden suggests he intended them to be read, they become an unstable, chimerical experiment in narrative and form, a collection of sometimes contradictory and half-formed voices and ideas that are assembled and reassembled in an attempt to advocate the trade as a component of a grander vision of English expansionism. This instability reflects their composition at a point of crisis. One example is Eden's compulsion to control narrative time. His repeated assertion of the inevitability of Pinteado's tragedy before the fleet had even departed and his description of himself surrounded with the spoils of Lok's voyage before his narrative had brought Lok's ships home are both responses to the prevailing atmosphere of threat and uncertainty that had engulfed that vision under the reign of his dedicatees Mary and Philip. It was an atmosphere that soon engulfed Eden, forcing him out of his Treasury job following accusations of heresy and into more precarious employment thereafter (Gwyn, 1984: 30–1).

Eden's sixteenth-century readers, many of whom read these accounts at a later point when the Guinea trade had flourished and England's seaborne mercantile expansion was fully underway, seem to have found the accounts more compelling than challenging. Their currency lasted for only a limited time, however. With his 1577 extended edition Richard Willes established Eden's book as foundational to a newly invigorated push to build his archive of English expansionism. So 'hyghly he was to be commended', Willes wrote in his preface, 'for Englyshyng so straunge, so wonderfull, so profitable histories as these are, nothyng inferior to the bookes of auncient writers, far exceedyng the multitude of foolysh commentaries and frivolous translations, to[o] to[o] licentiousely used in our tyme' (Willes, 1577: ℂ5v). The two Guinea voyages remained, with the aggressively anti-Wyndham tone of the first gently mollified, and they took on a yet greater significance as the originary point of a prospering trading enterprise. They had other impacts too. Eden's determination to produce voyage accounts that gained authenticity from those directly involved and were presented (at least in part) in the 'sorte and phrase of speache' as it was 'commonly used' among mariners (Eden, 1555: 349v) anticipated, even in some measure produced, what David Beers Quinn has identified as a late sixteenth-century flourish of prestige in which the heroic English sailor became a nationally celebrated figure (Quinn, 1974: 222–5).

Willes's edition certainly enhanced the continuing prominence of Eden's Guinea accounts, in part because it he was pitching it to a public already engaged in new English enterprises through Humphrey Gilbert's *A discourse of a discouerie for a new passage to Cataia* (1576) and Frobisher's first two voyages in search of that route, in 1576 and 1577 (Brennan, 1996/7: 238): indeed Willes had added his own discourse on 'M. Cap. Furbyshers Passage by the Northwest' to the edition, as noted on its title page. Those voyages generated a sequence of accounts and the obvious similarities between Eden's approach and Best's based on shared tone, sources (particularly Frisius), format, and preoccupations (climate, Indigenous customs, fauna) have already been mentioned. Others, even as they foregrounded the voice of the sailor, such as Thomas Ellis's *True report* (1578), followed a different model, one that often – like the Guinea voyage accounts of Robert Baker – involved considerable amounts of verse (Hakluyt, 1589: 130–42). Eden's example had evidently not restricted subsequent writers' generic options. By the time Hakluyt's *Principal Navigations* appeared in 1589, complete with Willes's version of Eden's two voyage accounts, however, a published form began to dominate that demonstrates Eden's influence. That debt was in part typographical: the marshalling and precise formatting of supporting documentary evidence, especially letters; the copious use of marginalia as a means of emphasis. It also consisted in Eden's pioneering incorporation of logbook material, his recognition of the value to readers of the voice of the mariner, and his willingness to editorialise where necessary. Hakluyt (and later Purchas) differed from Eden in his fundamental editorial method: for him 'documents themselves make truth claims', not their editor (Carey, 2019: 537). Eden's approach was much more flagrantly interventionist. Documents and testimony were absorbed, reformed, and reframed in order that the editor/author could produce truth. This differing approach begins to explain how Hakluyt's reformatting of the Guinea accounts further complicated their authorship. The documents were cut directly from Willes's 1577 edition of the *Decades* and required to stand for themselves: they retained the distinctive first-person voice of the original but identified Eden only as the author of the 'breefe description of Affrike'. Hakluyt also introduced running heads to identify and differentiate the voyages, which have subsequently (and mistakenly) been assumed to indicate authorship. Unwittingly he initiated a process that would eventually dissociate Eden from his own words. For Hakluyt, as for Willes, however, the primary value of these accounts lay not in their form or authorship but rather in the concrete evidence they presented on the nature and establishment of the English trade in West Africa. It was for the same reason that William Warner referenced them in 1592 and why Hakluyt prominently retained them (despite restructuring his material and discarding the Guinea accounts of Baker and William Huddie) for his second, extended edition.

It seems that once enshrined in Hakluyt's volume the frequency with which Eden's Wyndham and Lok accounts were referenced began to sharply wane. Because they were extraneous to Martyr's original *Decades* they did not feature in Michael Lok's new English translation (still in part based on Eden), *De novo orbe, or the historie of the west Indies* (1612), reissued in 1625 and 1628 (see Brennan, 1996/7: 241).[31] Although Samuel Purchas did reference the voyages in the first and subsequent editions of *Purchas his Pilgrimage*, he heavily compressed them (Purchas, 1613: 540–1), referring a reader back to Hakluyt for further detail, and they do not feature at all in his huge, multivolume *Purchas his Pilgrimes* (1625), displaced by translations of Portuguese material and later, more detailed English accounts. The centrality Eden had given West Africa to the narrative of early English commercial enterprise would remain for at least another century, even as his narratives were being reconstituted into more benign forms (as in *Golden Coast*, 1665: 20), but they were eventually displaced by different histories with different, imperial coordinates.

Although the currency of the two early Guinea accounts began to dip by the late seventeenth century, the generic form of the printed voyage of exploration Eden had pioneered was proliferating wildly. By the early eighteenth century its ubiquity was such that it was ripe for ridicule. So, when Richard Sympson, the fictional editor of Lemuel Gulliver's *Travels* and a kind of anti-Eden, introduced his readers to that text, he began with an apology. He warned of the plainness and simplicity of what was to come and of the tendency of his author to be 'a

---

[31] The title page of Lok's edition indicates that three of the original *Decades* 'have beene formerly translated into English, by *R. Eden*, whereunto the other five, are newly added by the Industrie, and painefull Travaile of *M. Lok* Gent' (Lok, 1612: title page).

little too Circumstantial': apparently a common failing amongst writers of travel. Furthermore, he writes:

> This Volume would have been at least twice as large, if I had not made bold to strike out innumerable Passages relating to the Winds and the Tides, as well as to the Variations and Bearings in the several Voyages; together with the minute Descriptions of the Management of the Ship in Storms, in the Style of Sailors. (Swift, 2001: 9–10)

Those disappointed by this caveat were reassured by Sympson's promise to provide 'the work at large, as it came from the Hand of the Author' if it were desired (Swift, 2001: 9). Despite all of this, Gulliver laments, still 'some of our Sea-*Yahoos* find Fault with my Sea-Language', as if he were some sort of fraud (Swift, 2001: 7).

Swift is scorning a mode of voyage writing that started in print with Richard Eden in 1555 and subsequently become central to English exploration writing (see Edwards, 1997). It is castigated for its endless authenticating gestures, for its obsessive cataloguing of irrelevant detail, and for its stylistic deficiencies; the latter a coded means to cast aspersions on its social status. For Swift, Gulliver's relatively humble beginnings and stubborn preoccupation with social hierarchies provided him a useful vantage from which to reflect on the cultures he observed on his travels, but they were also the cause of the simplicity and plainness of his writing. What for Eden guaranteed the authenticity of his two Guinea accounts became in the different circumstances of the late seventeenth and early eighteenth centuries a series of flaws, impediments to cultured reading and enjoyment.

This celebration of the absurdity of a genre Eden had initiated is the most eloquent indication of the scale of his success, for Swift's satirical attack on the staleness of the form implies the extraordinary abundance of accounts of exploration. They seemed to be everywhere. In *Gulliver's Travels*, for instance, the extreme lengths to which Swift goes to push his voyage account beyond authenticity and into the realms of satire (the paratextual notes from the publisher/editor and the disgruntled author, the conspicuously excised navigational data, the specially commissioned fake cartography) demonstrates how commonplace these kinds of devices had become since Eden's volume had first appeared. Indeed every one of the narrative devices Eden had reached for in recreating the two English Guinea voyages for print – melodrama, tragedy, self-reflection, polyvocality, disorienting shifts in scale and voice, as well as fore-grounding technical aspects through logbook-style detail – are present in some form in Swift's most famous work, which skewers paratextual posturing for publication just as much as it does the content of such texts. This was remarkable: what had begun as hastily assembled late additions to the English *Decades*, inserted to make a political point, to celebrate a new commercial endeavour, and to reach a general readership had somehow initiated a way of writing and thinking about voyages and exploration in print that had permeated English culture in less than two centuries. What had emerged from generic instability as fractured, contradictory accounts gathered and written for print by a conflicted figure at a time of religious and political crisis had, over time, through changing historical circumstance and repeated re-editing, been tamed and smoothed into coherence to become all-pervasive. Eden had therefore surely been right to trust that publication could resist creeping ignorance and the iniquities of time to preserve the memory of these voyages and initiate an archive of English expansionism. What neither he, his patrons, nor his early readers could have predicted was how the content of these accounts would swiftly and comprehensively be eclipsed by their form.

References

Manuscripts

Anon. (1557). New Years Guiftes. BL Add. MS 62525.

Francis Edwards to William Cecil (1560). NA SP 70/11/3.

Instructions to the Mayor of London (1555). NA PC 2/7 f. 283r.

Primary Sources

Al-Wazzan al-Fasi, A. (1600). *A geographical historie of Africa*. Trans. John Pory. London: George Bishop.

Anon. (1665). *The Golden coast, or, A description of Guinney*. London: S. Speed.

Arber, E. (1885). *The first three English books on America*. Birmingham: Turnbull & Spears.

Bacon, F. (1625). Of Travel. In F. Bacon, *The essayes or counsels, civill and morall*. London: John Havilland, pp. 100–4.

Bale, J. (1550). The apology of Iohan Bale agaynst a ranke papyst. London: John Day.

Best, G. (1578). *A true discourse of the late voyages of discoverie, for finding of a passage to Cathaya*. London: Henry Bynnyman.

Bibliander, T. (1542). *A godly consultation unto the brethren and companyons of the Christen religyon*. Antwerp: Radulphe Bonifante.

Cartier, J. (1545). *Brief récit de la navigation faicte és isles de Canada*. Paris: Ponce Roffet and Anthoine le Clerc.

de las Casas, B. (1552). *Brevisima relación de la desctrucción de las Indias*. Seville: Sebastian Trujillo.

de Castanheda, F. L. (1551–61). *Historia do descobrimento e conquista da India pelos Portuguezes*. Coimbra: por João da Barreira.

de Castanheda, F. L. (1582). *The first booke of the Historie of the discoverie and conquest of the East Indias*. London: Thomas East.

Eden, R. (1553). *A treatyse of the newe India, with other new founde landes and islandes*. London: Edward Sutton.

Eden, R. (1555). *The Decades of the Newe Worlde or West India*. London: William Powell.

Ellis, T. (1578). *A True Report of the Third and Last Voyage into Meta Incognita*. London: Thomas Dawson.

Frisius, G. (1530). *De Principiis Astronomiae & Cosmographiae*. Louvain and Antwerp: Servatium Zassenum and Gregorium Bontium.

Geuffroy, A. (1542). *The order of the greate Turckes courte*. London: Richard Grafton.

Gilbert, H. (1576). *A discourse of a discoverie for a new passage to Cataia*. London: Henry Middleton.

de Gómara, F. L. (1552). *Historia de las Indias y conquista de Mexico*. Saragossa: n.p.

Guilpin, E. (1598). *Skialetheia or, A shadowe of Truth*. London: James Roberts.

Hakluyt, R. (1589). *The principall navigations, voiages and discoveries of the English nation*. London: George Bishop and Ralph Newberie.

Hakluyt, R. (1598–1600). *The principal navigations, voiages, traffiques and discoveries of the English nation*. 3 vols. London: George Bishop, Ralph Newberie, and Robert Barker.

Lopes, D. (1597). *A report of the kingdome of Congo, a region of Africa*. London: John Wolfe.

Manuzio, A. (1543). *Viaggi fatti da Vinetia, alla Tana, in Persia, in India, et in Constantinopoli*. Venice: Aldo.

Martyr, P. (1612). *De novo orbe*, trans. M. Lok. London: Thomas Adams.

Münster, S. (1552). *Geographiae Claudii Ptolemaei Alexandrini*. Basle: H. Petri.

de Oviedo y Valdes, F. (1526). *La natural historia de las Indias*. Toledo: n.p.

de Oviedo y Valdes, F. (1535). *La historia general de las Indias*. Seville: Juan Cromberger.

Pigafetta, A. (1525). *Le voyage et navigation faict par les Espaignolz es Isles de Mollucques*. Paris: Simon de Colines.

Prat, W. (1554). *The discription of the contrey of Aphrique*. London: William Powell.

Purchas, S. (1613). *Purchas his Pilgrimage*. London: William Stansby.

Ramusio, G. B. (1550). *Della navigazioni e viaggi*. Venice: printed by the heirs of Lucantonio Giunti.

de Vaca, Á. Núñez Cabeza (1555). *Commentarios*. Valladolid: n.p.

di Varthema, L. (1510). *Itinerario*. Rome: Stephano Guillireti de Loreno and Hercule de Nani.

Warner, W. (1596). *Albions England a continued historie of the same kingdome*. London: Widow Orwin for Joan Broome.

Willes, R. (1577). *The history of travayle in the West and East Indies*. London: Richard Jugge.

de Xerez, F. (1534). *Verdadera relación de la conquista del Perù*. Seville: Bartolomé Perez.

de Zerate, A. (1555). *Historia del descubrimiento y conquista del Perù.* Antwerp: Martin Nucio.

Secondary Sources

Alsop, J. D. (1992). The Career of William Towerson, Guinea Trader. *International Journal of Maritime History* 4.2, 45–82.

Alsop, J. D. (2009). Wyndham, Thomas (d. 1554). Oxford Dictionary of National Biography. [accessed 06/03/20]

Andrea, B. (2016). 'Travelling Bodyes': Native Women of the Northeast and Northwest Passage Ventures and English Discourses of Empire. In A. Loomba and M. Sanchez eds., *Rethinking Feminism in Early Modern Studies.* London: Routledge, pp. 135–48.

Andrews, K. R. (1984). *Trade, Plunder and Settlement: Maritime Enterprise and the Genesis of the British Empire, 1480–1630.* Cambridge: Cambridge University Press.

Bassani, E., and W. B. Fagg (1988). *Africa and the Renaissance: Art in Ivory.* New York: The Center for African Art and Prestel-Verlag.

Bean, R. (1974). A Note on the Relative Importance of Slaves and Gold in West African Exports. *Journal of African History* 15.3, 351–6.

Blake, J. W. ed. (1942). *Europeans in West Africa 1540–1560,* vol. 2. London: The Hakluyt Society.

Brennan, M. G. (1996/7). The Texts of Peter Martyr's *De orbe novo decades* (1504–1628): A Response to Andrew Hadfield. *Connotations* 6.2, 227–45.

Brenner, R. (2003). *Merchants and Revolution: Commercial Change, Political Conflict, and London's Overseas Traders.* London: Verso.

Brooks, G. E. (2018 ed.). *Landlords and Strangers: Ecology, Society, and Trade in Western Africa, 1000–1630.* London: Routledge.

Carey, D. (2019). The Problem of Credibility in Early Modern Travel. *Renaissance Studies* 33.4, 524–47.

Casale, G. (2010). *The Ottoman Age of Exploration.* Oxford: Oxford University Press.

Cell, G. C. (1969). *English Enterprise in Newfoundland 1577–1660.* Toronto: Toronto University Press.

Chaney, E. (1998). *The Evolution of the Grand Tour: Anglo-Italian Cultural Relations since the Renaissance.* London: Frank Cass.

Cummings, B. (2004). Pliny's Literate Elephant and the Idea of Animal Language in Renaissance Thought. In E. Fudge ed., *Renaissance Beasts: Of Animals, Humans, and Other Wonderful Creatures.* Urbana: University of Illinois Press, pp. 164–85.

Dalton, H. (2016). *Merchants and Explorers: Roger Barlow, Sebastian Cabot, and Networks of Atlantic Exchange 1500–1560*. Oxford: Oxford University Press.

Das, N. (2019). Early Modern Travel Writing (2): English Travel Writing. In N. Das and T. Youngs eds., *The Cambridge History of Travel Writing*. Cambridge: Cambridge University Press, pp. 77–92.

Davies, S. (2016). *Renaissance Ethnography and the Invention of the Human: New Worlds, Maps and Monsters*. Cambridge: Cambridge University Press.

Dimmock, M. (2019). *Elizabethan Globalism: England, China and the Rainbow Portrait*. New Haven, CT: Yale University Press for the Paul Mellon Centre.

Ebert, C. (2008). European Competition and Cooperation in Pre-modern Globalization: 'Portuguese' West and Central Africa, 1500–1600. *African Economic History* 36, 58–78.

Edwards, P. (1997). *Sea-mark: The Metaphorical Voyage, Spenser to Milton*. Liverpool: Liverpool University Press.

Fage, J. D. (1980). A Commentary on Duarte Pacheco Pereria's Account of the Lower Guinea Coastlands in His 'Esmeraldo de Situ Orbis', and in Some Other Early Accounts. *History in Africa* 7, 47–80.

Faldini, L. (1992). Peoples and Cultures of the New World. In G. E. Viola ed., *Columbian Iconography*. Rome: Insituto Poligrafico e Zecca Dello Strato, pp. 51–70.

Fitzmaurice, A. (2003). *Humanism and America: An Intellectual History of English Colonialisation, 1500–1625*. Cambridge: Cambridge University Press.

Floyd-Wilson, M. (2003). *English Ethnicity and Race in Early Modern Drama*. Cambridge: Cambridge University Press.

Fuller, M. C. (2006). Making something of it: Questions of value in the early English travel collection. *Journal of Early Modern History* 10 (1–2), 11–38.

Fuller, M. C. (2008). *Remembering the Early Modern Voyage: English Narratives in the Age of Expansion*. Basingstoke: Palgrave Macmillan.

Fuller, M. C. (2019). Afterword: Looking for the Women in Early Modern Travel Writing. In P. Akhimie and B. Andrea eds., *Travel and Travail: Early Modern Women, English Drama, and the Wider World*. Lincoln: University of Nebraska Press, pp. 331–52.

Garrard, T. F. (1982). Myth and Metrology: The Early Trans-Saharan Gold Trade. *The Journal of African History* 23.4, 443–61.

Greenblatt, S. (1991). *Marvelous Possessions: The Wonder of the New World*. Oxford: Clarendon.

Gwyn, D. (1984). Richard Eden: Cosmographer and Alchemist. *Sixteenth-Century Journal* 15, 13–34.

Hadfield, A. (1995/6). Peter Martyr, Richard Eden and the New World: Reading, Experience and Translation. *Connotations* 5.1, 1–22.

Hadfield, A. (1998). *Literature, Travel, and Colonial Writing in the English Renaissance, 1545–1625*. Oxford: Oxford University Press.

Hair, P. E. H. (1994). Early Sources on Guinea. *History in Africa* 21, 87–126.

Hair, P. E. H. (1997). The Experience of the Sixteenth-Century English Voyages to Guinea. *The Mariners Mirror* 83.1, 3–13.

Hair, P. E. H., and J. D. Alsop (1992). *English Seamen and Traders in Guinea 1553–1565: The New Evidence of Their Wills*. Lewiston: The Edwin Mellen Press.

Hall, K. F. (1995). *Things of Darkness: Economies of Race and Gender in Early Modern England*. Ithaca, NY: Cornell University Press.

Hecht, J. (2008). Ivory and Boxwood Carvings, 1450–1800. In *Heilbrunn Timeline of Art History*. New York: The Metropolitan Museum of Art: www.metmuseum.org/toah/hd/boxw/hd_boxw.htm (accessed 28/09/21).

Herodotus (1921 ed.). *The Persian Wars*, vol. 2, trans. A. D. Godley. Cambridge, MA: Harvard University Press [Loeb Classical Library].

Homer (1919 ed.). *Odyssey*, vol. 2, trans. A. T. Murray. Cambridge, MA: Harvard University Press [Loeb Classical Library].

Jones, A. (1986). *Semper Aliquid Veteris*: Printed Sources for the History of the Ivory and Gold Coasts, 1500–1750. *The Journal of African History* 27.2, 215–35.

Jones, E. T. (2000). England's Icelandic Fishery in the Early Modern Period. In D. J. Starkey, C. Reid, and N. Ashcroft eds., *England's Sea Fisheries: The Commercial Sea Fisheries of England and Wales since 1300*. London: Chatham. 105–110.

Kleist, A. M. (1957). The English African Trade under the Tudors. *Transactions of the Historical Society of Ghana* 3.2, 63–76.

Lawson, J. A. ed. (2013). *The Elizabethan New Year's Gift Exchanges, 1559–1603*. Oxford: Oxford University Press.

Madox, R. (1976). *An Elizabethan in 1582: The Diary of Richard Madox, Fellow of All Souls*, ed. Elizabeth Story Donno. London: The Hakluyt Society.

McDermott, J. (2001). *Martin Frobisher: Elizabethan Privateer*. New Haven, CT: Yale University Press.

de Montaigne, M. (2003 ed.). *The Complete Essays*, ed. M. A. Screech. London: Penguin.

Morgan, J. L. (2021). *Reckoning with Slavery: Gender, Kinship, and Capitalism in the Early Black Atlantic.* Durham, NC: Duke University Press.

Northrup, D. (2014 ed.). *Africa's Discovery of Europe, 1450–1850.* Oxford: Oxford University Press.

Olusoga, D. (2016). *Black and British: A Forgotten History.* London: Macmillan.

Ovid (1916 ed.). *Metamorphoses,* vol. 1, trans. Frank Justus Miller. Cambridge, MA: Harvard University Press [Loeb Classical Library].

Palmer, P. S. (2013). 'All Suche matters as passed on this vyage': Early English Travel Anthologies and the Case of John Sarracoll's Maritime Journal (1586–87). *Huntington Library Quarterly* 76.3, 325–44.

Penrose, B. (1955). *Travel and Discovery in the Renaissance, 1420–1620.* Cambridge, MA: Harvard University Press.

Porter, H. C. (1979). *The Inconstant Savage: England and the North American Indian, 1500–1660.* London: Duckworth.

Quinn, D. B. (1974). *England and the Discovery of America, 1481–1620.* New York: Alfred A. Knopf.

Rastell, J. (1979). *Three Rastell Plays: Four Elements, Calisto, and Melebea, Gentleness and Nobility,* ed. Richard Axton. Cambridge: D. S. Brewer.

de la Rosa, A. C. (2002). Representing the New World's Nature: Wonder and Exoticism in Gonzalo Fernández de Oviedo y Valdes. *Historical Reflections* 28.1, 73–92.

Rublack, U. (2010). *Dressing Up: Cultural Identity in Renaissance Europe.* Oxford: Oxford University Press.

Ryder, A. F. C. (1969). *Benin and the Europeans, 1485–1897.* London: Longman.

Salvadore, M. (2010). The Ethiopian Age of Exploration: Prester John's Discovery of Europe, 1306–1458. *Journal of World History* 21.4, 593–627.

Schotte, M. (2013). Expert Records: Nautical Logbooks from Columbus to Cook. *Information & Culture* 48.3, 281–322.

Sell, J. P. A. (2006). *Rhetoric and Wonder in English Travel Writing, 1560–1613.* Aldershot: Ashgate.

Sherman, W. H. (1995). *John Dee: The Politics of Reading and Writing in the English Renaissance.* Amherst: University of Massachusetts Press.

Sherman, W. H. (2002). Stirrings and Searchings (1500–1720). In P. Hulme and T. Youngs eds., *The Cambridge Companion to Travel Writing.* Cambridge: Cambridge University Press, pp. 17–36.

Shumway, R. (2011a). The Fante Shrine of Nananom Mpow and the Atlantic Slave Trade in Southern Ghana. *The International Journal of African Historical Studies* 44.1, 27–44.

Shumway, R. (2011b). *The Fante and the Transatlantic Slave Trade.* Rochester, NY: University of Rochester Press.

Silverberg, R. (1996 ed.). *The Realm of Prester John.* Athens: Ohio University Press.

Small, M. (2012). A World Seen through Another's Eyes: Hakluyt, Ramusio, and the Narratives of the *Navigationi et Viaggi.* In D. Carey and C. Jowitt eds., *Richard Hakluyt and Travel Writing in Early Modern Europe.* Farnham: Ashgate, pp. 45–55.

Stoye, J. (1989 ed.). *English Travellers Abroad, 1604–1667: Their Influence in English Society and Politics.* New Haven, CT: Yale University Press.

Sullivan, A. (2020). *Britain's War against the Slave Trade: The Operations of the Royal Navy's West Africa Squadron 1807–1867.* Barnsley: Pen & Sword.

Swift, J. (2001 ed.). *Gulliver's Travels*, ed. Robert DeMaria Jr. London: Penguin Classics.

Thornton, J. (1998 ed.). *Africa and Africans in the Making of the Atlantic World, 1400–1800.* Cambridge: Cambridge University Press.

Vaughan, A. T. (2006). *Transatlantic Encounters: American Indians in Britain, 1500–1776.* Cambridge: Cambridge University Press.

Vaughan A. T., and V. M. Vaughan (1997). Before *Othello*: Elizabethan Representations of Sub-Saharan Africans. *The William and Mary Quarterly* 54.1, 19–44.

Wernham, R. B. (1966). *Before the Armada: The Growth of English Foreign Policy, 1485–1588.* London: Jonathan Cape.

Willan, T. S. (1953). *The Muscovy Merchants of 1555.* Manchester: Manchester University Press.

Williamson J. A. (1962 ed.). *The Cabot Voyages and Bristol Discovery under Henry VII.* Cambridge: Cambridge University Press for the Hakluyt Society.

Young, S. (2015). *The Early Modern Global South in Print: Textual Form and the Production of Human Difference As Knowledge.* London: Routledge.

Zemon Davis, N. (2007). *Trickster Travels: In Search of Leo Africanus, A Sixteenth-Century Muslim between Worlds.* London: Faber.

Cambridge Elements ☰

Travel Writing

Nandini Das
University of Oxford

Nandini Das is a literary scholar and cultural historian, professor of early modern literature and culture at the University of Oxford, and fellow of Exeter College, Oxford. With Tim Youngs, she has co-edited *The Cambridge History of Travel Writing* (2019) and published widely on early modern English literature, cross-cultural encounters, and travel accounts.

Tim Youngs
Nottingham Trent University

Tim Youngs is Professor of English and Travel Studies at Nottingham Trent University. His books include *The Cambridge Companion to Travel Writing* (edited with Peter Hulme, 2002), *The Cambridge Introduction to Travel Writing* (2013), and *The Cambridge History of Travel Writing* (edited with Nandini Das, 2019). He edits the journal *Studies in Travel Writing*.

About the Series

Travel writing is enormously varied. It consists of several different forms and has a long history across many cultures. This series aims to reflect that diversity, offering exciting studies of a range of travel texts and topics. The Elements further advance the latest thinking in travel writing, extending previous work and opening up the field to fresh readings and subjects of inquiry.

Cambridge Elements ≡

Travel Writing

Elements in the Series

Eco-Travel: Journeying in the Age of the Anthropocene
Michael Cronin

Writing Tudor Exploration: Richard Eden and West Africa
Matthew Dimmock

A full series listing is available at: www.cambridge.org/ELTW

Printed in the United States
by Baker & Taylor Publisher Services